A POEM A DAY

ORCHARD BOOKS
96 Leonard Street, London EC2A 4XD
Orchard Books Australia
Unit 31/56 O'Riordan Street, Alexandria, NSW 2015
ISBN 1 84121 741 7
First published in Great Britain in 2001
Text selection © Adrian Mitchell 2001
Illustrations copyright: pp10–81 © Russell Ayto 2001, pp148–215 © Peter Bailey 2001,
pp82–147 © Lauren Child 2001, pp216–281 © Guy Parker-Rees 2001
The rights of Adrian Mitchell to be identified as the compiler
and of Russell Ayto, Peter Bailey, Lauren Child and Guy Parker-Rees
to be identified as the illustrators have been asserted by them in
accordance with the Copyright, Designs and Patents Act, 1988.
A CIP catalogue record for this book is available from the British Library.
3 5 7 9 10 8 6 4 2
Printed in Hong Kong

A POEM A DAY

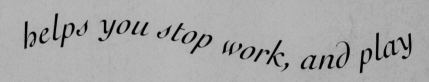

helps you stop work, and play

Chosen by
Adrian Mitchell

Illustrated by
Russell Ayto, Peter Bailey,
Lauren Child and Guy Parker-Rees

ORCHARD BOOKS

for my grandchildren –
    Robin, Lola, Zoe, Arthur, Caitlin, Charlotte and Natasha
for my children –
    Beattie, Sasha, Briony, Danny and Alistair
for my adopted daughter –
    Boty Goodwin
for my wife –
    Celia
for my brother –
    Jimmy
and all his family
and for our parents –
    Kathleen and Jock
A M

for Alyx
R A

for Siân, Owain and Anwen
P B

for my friend Kate Valentine
love Lauren

to Sian and Laura
G P-R

A birthday book for a 367-day year

✳ 367 DAYS IN A YEAR?

Aren't there only 365 usually? And 366 in a Leap Year? That's true, but poetry is a generous place, so you get an extra day, if you can find it.

✳ THE SHAPE OF THE BOOK

On every date we've printed a poem or part of a poem to treasure. Some were written by great poets, some were made up by children in playgrounds. Look up the poem on your own birthday – it's as reliable a method of foretelling the future as any other!

✳ THE POEM HUNT

I wandered through hundreds of books of poetry,
looking for verses which spoke
    Clearly, wisely and wittily,
    Wildly, scarily, and prettily.
    I found some fantastical,
    Or dug up some real,
    And mixed in nonsensical
    To make a varied meal . . .

* OLD-FASHIONED? WHY NOT?

This book was made to last, not built for speed. That's why you won't find many up-to-date, topical or fashionable poems in it. If I'd tried to be cool and chic etc, with references to cellphones and downloading robots and digital crocodile bytes and airplane meals with trayfuls of bits and pieces encased in plastic which you can't break open without a laser gun – the book would have been obsolete before it could be printed. But I want this book to last till the next millennium. And poems about animals and trees and love will always make some sort of sense.

Many of the poets in this book are dead. I'm sorry about that, but most of the greatest poets are dead. They can't help it.

I've chosen writers whose poems speak in living language. Christina Rossetti, William Blake, Emily Dickinson, John Clare and William Shakespeare are among those who can become your lifelong, amazing friends.

* WHEN'S YOUR POETRY BIRTHDAY?

If the poem which falls on your Birthday date
Is one you don't like or even hate –
Jump six days on. No? Another six
Until you find the poem that clicks.
That's your Poetry Birthday. On that date
Write a poem for your parents
    and your best mate,
For your sisters and brothers,
    your dog and your cat.
When they ask you why, simply tell them that
IT'S MY POETRY BIRTHDAY!
    Smile and look pleasant –
You never know –
    someone might give you a present.

A poem a day keeps the grey away.

*And, just before you start
    looking up your own birthday –*

The World
Wants To Welcome You

I'm your old rock cake, your old cream bun
And I'm a-travelling round the sun.
I ain't got a clue where I am bound
But I sings to myself as I trundle round:

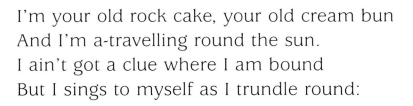

I starts my journey in January,
Now that's an old habit I never do vary
And next I sloshes through February
Though the rain be rough and the hail be hairy.

I battles my way through the winds of March
And out through a magical rainbow arch
Into the country of April
With her showers and flowers on every little hill.

Then off I dances to the land of May
Watching young otters and mice at play
And over the giddy goats of June
I sails like a happy old balloon.

Watch me spinning across July
Chasing a flutterby butterfly.
In the seaside season of August
I gets no holiday but I'm not fussed

As I bounces into the club of September
Where I'm greeted as the oldest member
And on I rolls into golden October –
I drinks his wine but I stays sober.

I stumbles through the mists of smoky Novembers,
And warm my mittens at the bonfire's embers.
I races with Santa's sleigh over December –
Surely I've been here before? I remember!

    I'm your old rock cake, your old cream bun
    And I'm a-travelling round the sun.
    I ain't got a clue where I am bound
    But I sings to myself as I trundle round.

ADRIAN MITCHELL

January 1

Almost Unbreakable New Year's Resolution

I will look through my eyes,
    Write with my hand
And walk, usually, on my feet.
I will breathe some breaths
    Each and every day
To encourage my heart to beat.

I will eat some food,
    I will drink some drink
And maybe, just now and then,
    Sit down and think.

ADRIAN MITCHELL

January 2

An emerald is as green as grass,
    A ruby red as blood;
A sapphire shines as blue as heaven;
    A flint lies in the mud.

A diamond is a brilliant stone,
    To catch the world's desire;
An opal holds a fiery spark;
    But a flint holds fire.

CHRISTINA ROSSETTI

January 3

Trudging

The night was growing old
    As she trudged through snow and sleet;
And her nose was long and cold,
    And her shoes were full of feet.

ANON

January 4

Stopping by Woods on a Snowy Evening

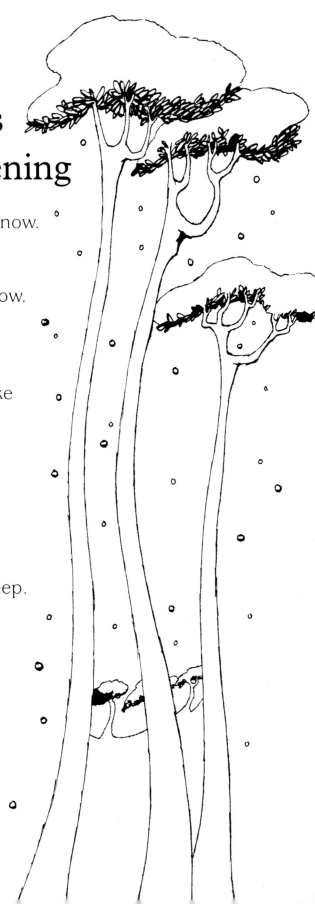

Whose woods these are I think I know.
His house is in the village though;
He will not see me stopping here
To watch his woods fill up with snow.

My little horse must think it queer
To stop without a farmhouse near
Between the woods and frozen lake
The darkest evening of the year.

He gives his harness bells a shake
To ask if there is some mistake.
The only other sound's the sweep
Of easy wind and downy flake.

The woods are lovely, dark and deep.
But I have promises to keep,
And miles to go before I sleep,
And miles to go before I sleep.

ROBERT FROST

January 5

I Saw

I saw a peacock with a fiery tail
I saw a blazing comet pour down hail
I saw a cloud wrapped with ivy round
I saw an oak creeping upon the ground
I saw an ant swallow up a whale
I saw the sea brimful of ale
I saw a Venice glass fifteen feet deep
I saw a well full of men's tears that weep
I saw wet eyes all of a flaming fire
I saw a horse bigger than the moon and higher
I saw the sun even at midnight
I saw the man who saw this dreadful sight.

ANON

January 6

Buffalo Dusk

The buffaloes are gone.
And those who saw the buffaloes are gone.
Those who saw the buffaloes by thousands and
    how they pawed the prairie sod into dust
    with their hoofs, their great heads down
    pawing on in a great pageant of dusk,
Those who saw the buffaloes are gone.
And the buffaloes are gone.

CARL SANDBURG

January 7

from Auguries of Innocence

To see a World in a grain of sand,
And a Heaven in a wild flower,
Hold Infinity in the palm of your hand,
And Eternity in an hour.

A robin redbreast in a cage
Puts all Heaven in a rage.
A dove-house fill'd with doves and pigeons
Shudders Hell thro' all its regions.

A dog starv'd at his master's gate
Predicts the ruin of the State.
A horse misus'd upon the road
Calls to Heaven for human blood.

Each outcry from the hunted hare
A fibre from the brain does tear.
A skylark wounded in the wing,
A cherubim does cease to sing.

WILLIAM BLAKE

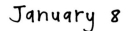

January 8

Sally

Sally go round the sun,
    Sally,
Sally go round the moon,
Sally go round the ombelibus
On a Saturday afternoon.

ANON

January 9

All Over the Lilac Brine!

Around the shores of the Arrogant Isles,
Where the Cat-fish bask and purr,
And lick their paws with adhesive smiles,
And wriggle their fins of fur,

With my wife in a dress of mustard-and-cress,
On a table of rare design,
We skim and we fly, 'neath a fourpenny sky,
All over the lilac brine.

MERVYN PEAKE

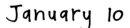

January 10

A Roost on the Rim of the World

I seen a owl settin'
On the rim of the moon.
He draw in he neck, an' rumple he feather,
An' look below at the world.
He shook the horns on he head,
An' laugh at the things above an' below,
From he roost on the rim of the moon.

ANON

January 11

The Animal Fair

We went to the Animal Fair,
The birds and the beasts were there.
The big baboon by the light of the moon
Was combing his auburn hair.

The monkey fell out of his bunk
Right on to the elephant's trunk,
The elephant sneezed and fell on his knees
And what became of the monkey,
Monkey, monkey, monkey, monk?

ANON

January 12

Four Liam for Liam

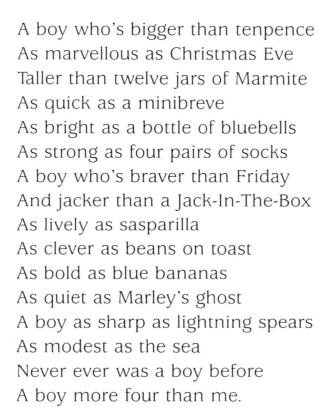

A boy who's bigger than tenpence
As marvellous as Christmas Eve
Taller than twelve jars of Marmite
As quick as a minibreve
As bright as a bottle of bluebells
As strong as four pairs of socks
A boy who's braver than Friday
And jacker than a Jack-In-The-Box
As lively as sasparilla
As clever as beans on toast
As bold as blue bananas
As quiet as Marley's ghost
A boy as sharp as lightning spears
As modest as the sea
Never ever was a boy before
A boy more four than me.

WILLY RUSSELL

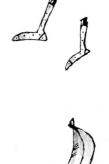

January 13

from Address to a Child during a Boisterous Winter Evening

What way does the Wind come? What way does he go?
He rides over the water, and over the snow,
Through wood, and through vale; and o'er rocky height,
Which the goat cannot climb, takes his sounding flight;
He tosses about in every bare tree,
As, if you look up, you may plainly see;
But how he will come, and whither he goes,
There's never a scholar in England knows.

DOROTHY WORDSWORTH

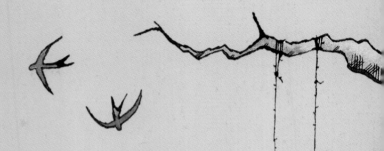

January 14

from Past and Present

I remember, I remember,
The house where I was born,
The little window where the sun
Came peeping in at morn;
He never came a wink too soon,
Nor brought too long a day,
But now, I often wish the night
Had borne my breath away.

I remember, I remember,
Where I was used to swing,
And thought the air must rush as fresh
To swallows on the wing;
My spirit flew in feathers then,
That is so heavy now,
And summer pools could hardly cool
The fever on my brow.

THOMAS HOOD

January 15

He who owns the whistle, rules the World

january wind and the sun
playing truant again.
Rain beginning to scratch
its fingernails across
the blackboard sky

in the playground
kids divebomb, corner
at silverstone or execute
traitors. Armed
with my Acme Thunderer
I step outside,
take a deep breath
and bring the world
to a standstill

ROGER MCGOUGH

January 16

Little Husband

I had a little husband,
    No bigger than my thumb.
I put him in a jampot,
    Told him to beat his drum.
I found a friendly beetle
    To knit him woolly clothes
And sew a little handkerchief
    To wipe his dirty nose.

ANON

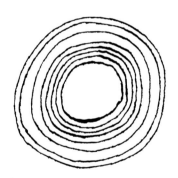

January 17

Shine Out, Fair Sun

Shine out, fair sun, with all your heat,
Show all your thousand-coloured light!
Black winter freezes to his seat;
The grey wolf howls he does so bite;
Crookt age on three knees creeps the street;
The boneless fish close quaking lies
And eats for cold his aching feet;
The stars in icicles arise:
Shine out, and make this winter night
Our beauty's spring, Our Prince of Light!

ANON

January 18

Sheep in Winter

The sheep get up and make their many tracks
And bear a load of snow upon their backs,
And gnaw the frozen turnip to the ground
With sharp quick bite, and then go noising round
The boy that pecks the turnips all the day
And knocks his hand to keep the cold away
And laps his legs in straw to keep them warm
And hides behind the hedges from the storm.
The sheep, as tame as dogs, go where he goes
And try to shake their fleeces from the snows,
Then leave their frozen meal and wander round
The stubble stack that stands beside the ground,
And lie all night and face the drizzling storm
And shun the hovel where they might be warm.

JOHN CLARE

January 19

Infant Innocence

The Grizzly Bear is huge and wild;
He has devoured the infant child.
The infant child is not aware
He has been eaten by the bear.

A. E. HOUSMAN

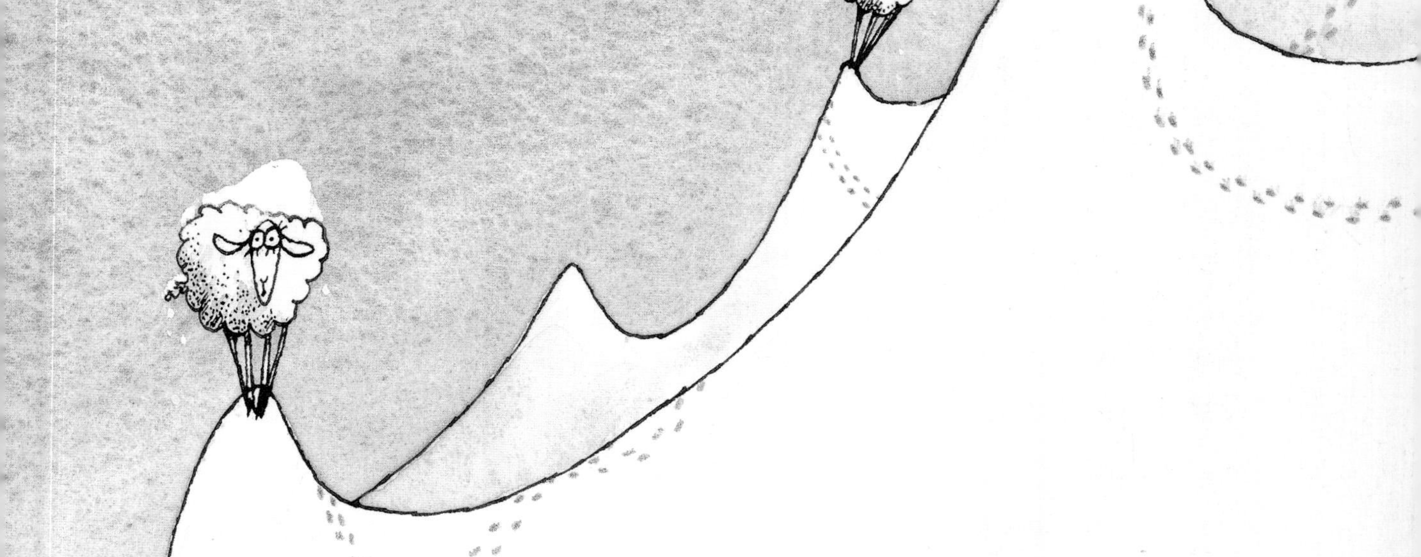

January 20

The Last of Mary Ann

Mary Ann has gone to rest,
Safe at last on Abraham's breast,
Which may be nuts for Mary Ann,
But is certainly rough on Abraham.

ANON

January 21

The Moon

The moon has a face like the clock in the hall;
She shines on thieves on the garden wall,
On streets and fields and harbour quays,
And birdies asleep in the forks of the trees.

The squalling cat and the squeaking mouse,
The howling dog by the door of the house,
The bat that lies in bed at noon,
All love to be out by the light of the moon.

But all of the things that belong to the day
Cuddle to sleep to be out of her way;
And flowers and children close their eyes
Till up in the morning the sun shall rise.

ROBERT LOUIS STEVENSON

January 22

So We'll Go No More A Roving

So, we'll go no more a roving
    So late into the night,
Though the heart be still as loving,
    And the moon be still as bright.

For the sword outwears its sheath,
    And the soul wears out the breast,
And the heart must pause to breathe,
    And love itself have rest.

Though the night was made for loving,
    And the day returns too soon,
Yet we'll go no more a roving
    By the light of the moon.

GEORGE GORDON BYRON

January 23

Winter

When icicles hang by the wall
    And Dick the shepherd blows his nail,
And Tom bears logs into the hall,
    And milk comes frozen home in pail;
When blood is nipt, and ways be foul,
Then nightly sings the staring owl
    Tu-whoo!
To-whit, Tu-whoo! A merry note!
While greasy Joan doth keel the pot.

When all about the wind doth blow,
    And coughing drowns the parson's saw,
And birds sit brooding in the snow,
    And Marian's nose looks red and raw;
When roasted crabs hiss in the bowl –
Then nightly sings the staring owl
    Tu-whoo!
To-whit, Tu-whoo! A merry note!
While greasy Joan doth keel the pot.

WILLIAM SHAKESPEARE, FROM *LOVE'S LABOURS LOST*

January 24

The Sound of the Wind

The wind has such a rainy sound
    Moaning through the town,
The sea has such a windy sound –
    Will the ships go down?

The apples in the orchard
    Tumble from their tree –
Oh, will the ships go down, go down,
    In the windy sea?

CHRISTINA ROSSETTI

January 25

Whistle, An' I'll Come to Ye, My Lad

O whistle, an' I'll come to ye, my lad;
O whistle, an' I'll come to ye, my lad;
Though father and mither should baith gae mad,
Thy Jeannie will venture wi ye, my lad.

Come down the back stairs when ye come to court me;
Come down the back stairs when ye come to court me;
Come down the back stairs, and let naebody see;
And come as ye were na coming to me –
And come as ye were na coming to me.

ROBERT BURNS

January 26

A London Tragedy

A muvver was barfin' 'er biby one night,
The youngest of ten and a tiny young mite,
The muvver was poor and the biby was thin,
Only a skellington covered in skin;
The muvver turned rahnd for the soap off the rack,
She was but a moment, but when she turned back,
The biby was gorn! And in anguish she cried,
"Oh, where is my biby?" – The Angels replied:

"Your biby 'as fell dahn the plug-'ole,
Your biby 'as gorn dahn the plug;
The poor little fing was so scroony and thin
'E oughter bin barfed in a jug;
Your biby is perfickly 'appy,
'E won't need a barf any more.
Your biby what fell dahn the plug-'ole,
Is not lorst, but gorn before."

ANON

January 27

Jabberwocky

'Twas brillig, and the slithy toves
   Did gyre and gimble in the wabe:
All mimsy were the borogroves,
   And the mome raths outgrabe.

"Beware the Jabberwock, my son!
   The jaws that bite, the claws that catch!
Beware the Jubjub bird and shun
   The frumious Bandersnatch!"

He took his vorpal sword in hand:
   Long time the manxome foe he sought –
So rested he by the Tumtum tree,
   And stood awhile in thought.

And, as in uffish thought he stood,
   The Jabberwock, with eyes of flame,
Came whiffling through the tulgey wood,
   And burbled as it came!

One, two! One, two! And through and through
   The vorpal blade went snicker-snack!
He left it dead, and with its head
   He went galumphing back.

"And hast thou slain the Jabberwock?
    Come to my arms, my beamish boy!
O frabjous day! Callooh! Callay!"
    He chortled in his joy.

'Twas brillig, and the slithy toves
    Did gyre and gimble in the wabe:
All mimsy were the borogroves,
    And the mome raths outgrabe.

LEWIS CARROLL

January 28

A Norrible Day

Yesterday was a norrible day and there was such a lot of it.
Yesterday was a norful day I wish I could get shot of it.
But yesterday was yesterday – pull the chain and flush it away!
    Hooray!

ADRIAN MITCHELL

January 29

Counting Out Rhyme

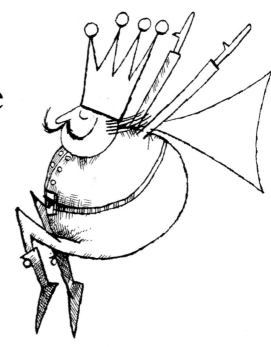

Zeenty, peenty, heathery, mithery,
Bumfy, leery, over, Dover,
Saw the King of Heazle Peazle
Jumping o'er Jerusalem Dyke:
    Black fish, white trout
    Eenie, ourie, you're out!

ANON

January 30

from Hurricane 1951

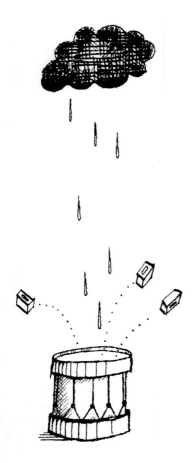

I remember the night,
black with slack rain,
flaccid when it first began
but with brick drops beating later on
like jump-Poco drumthumps,
beating back the coming morning,
beating with purpose,
routine, rhythm and ritual,
beating like the bounce of batter hide,
hide battered on a shoemaker's block,
batter hide, hide battered,
pane shatter, shattered pane,
batter hide, pane shatter through to dawn.

ANDREW SALKEY

January 31

from Summer

Winter is cold-hearted,
    Spring is yea and nay,
Autumn is a weathercock
    Blown every way:
Summer days for me
When every leaf is on the tree;

When Robin's not a beggar,
    And Jenny Wren's a bride,
And larks hang singing, singing, singing,
    Over the wheatfields wide,
    And anchored lilies ride,
And the pendulum spider
    Swings from side to side.

CHRISTINA ROSSETTI

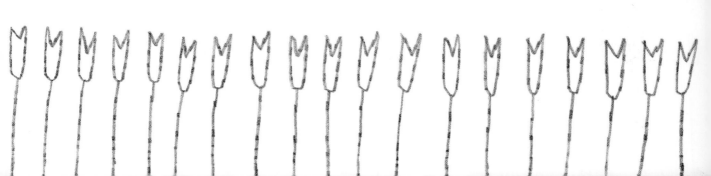

February 1

My Horse Named Bill

Oh I had a horse and his name was Bill,
And when he ran he couldn't stand still.
He ran away – one day – and also I ran with him.

He ran so fast he could not stop,
He ran into a barber shop,
And fell exhaustionized – with his eyeteeth –
In the barber's left shoulder.

Oh, I went up in a balloon so big,
The people on earth they looked like a pig,
Like a mice – like a katydid – like flieses – and like fleasens.
The balloon turned up with its bottom side higher,
It fell on the wife of a country squire,
She made a noise like a dog hound, like a steam whistle
And also like dynamite.

Oh what could you do in a case like that?
Oh what could you do but stamp on your hat,
And your toothbrush – and everything – that's helpless!

ANON

34

February 2

Fame

The best thing
about being famous

is when you walk
down the street

and people turn round
to look at you

and bump into things.

ROGER MCGOUGH

February 3

Familiar Love Story

There was a lady loved a swine,
 Honey, quoth she,
Pig-hog wilt thou be mine?
 Hoogh, quoth he.

I'll build thee a silver sty,
 Honey, quoth she,
And in it thou shalt lie.
 Hoogh, quoth he.

Pinned with a silver pin,
 Honey, quoth she,
That thou may go out and in.
 Hoogh, quoth he.

Wilt thou have me now,
 Honey? quoth she,
Speak, or my heart will break.
 Hoogh, quoth he.

ANON

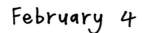

February 4

A Rhyme
to Say to a Scottish Bat

Arymouse, arymouse, fly over my head,
And you shall ha' a crust o' bread;
And when I brew and when I bake,
You shall ha' a piece of my wedding-cake.

ANON

February 5

Snow

In the gloom of whiteness,
In the great silence of snow,
A child was sighing
And bitterly saying: 'Oh,
They have killed a white bird up there on her nest,
The down is fluttering from her breast!'
And still it fell through that dusky brightness
On the child crying for the bird of the snow.

EDWARD THOMAS

February 6

from Kangaroo

Delicate mother Kangaroo
Sitting up there rabbit-wise, but huge, plumb-weighted,
And lifting her beautiful slender face, oh! so much more gently
    and finely lined than a rabbit's, or than a hare's,
Lifting her face to nibble at a round white peppermint drop,
    which she loves, sensitive mother Kangaroo.

Her sensitive, long, pure-bred face.
Her full antipodal eyes, so dark,
So big and quiet and remote, having watched so many empty
    dawns in silent Australia.

Her little loose hands, and drooping Victorian shoulders.
And then her great weight below the waist, her vast pale belly
With a thin young yellow little paw hanging out, and straggle
    of a long thin ear, like ribbon,
Like a funny trimming to the middle of her belly, thin little
    dangle of an immature paw, and one thin ear.

D. H. LAWRENCE

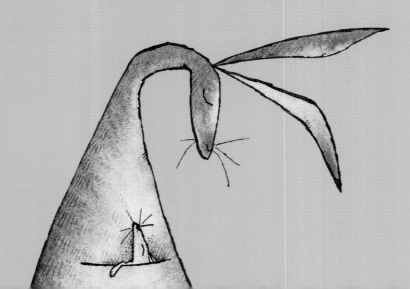

February 7

from Calico Pie

Calico Pie,
The little Birds fly
Down to the calico tree,
Their wings were blue,
And they sang 'Tilly-loo!'
Till away they flew, –
And they never came back to me!
They never came back!
They never came back!
They never came back to me!

EDWARD LEAR

February 8

from The Palace of Humbug

I dreamt I dwelt in marble halls,
And each damp thing that creeps and crawls
Went wobble-wobble on the walls.

Faint odours of departed cheese,
Blown on the dank, unwholesome breeze,
Awoke the never-ending sneeze.

LEWIS CARROLL

February 9

Mad Meals

Grilled cork
Matchbox on toast
glass soup
roasted clock
ping-pong ball and chips
Acorn sandwich
fillet of calculator
trouser salad
grilled lamp-post
ice-cream (vanilla, soap or pepper)

Mad Drinks

fizzy mouse
hot petrol
paint shake

MICHAEL ROSEN

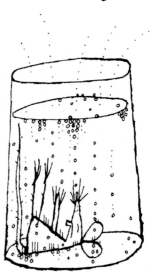

February 10

Queen Nefertiti

Spin a coin, spin a coin
    All fall down;
Queen Nefertiti
    Stalks through the town.

Over the pavements
    Her feet go clack.
Her legs are tall
    As a chimney stack.

Her fingers flicker
    Like snakes in the air,
The walls split open
    At her green-eyed stare.

Her voice is thin
    As the ghosts of bees,
She will crumble your bones,
    She will make your blood freeze.

Spin a coin, spin a coin,
    All fall down,
Queen Nefertiti
    Stalks through the town.

ANON

February 11

Squeezes

We love to squeeze bananas,
We love to squeeze ripe plums,
And when they are feeling sad
We love to squeeze our mums.

BRIAN PATTEN

February 12

The Tide in the River

The tide in the river,
The tide in the river,
The tide in the river runs deep,
I saw a shiver
Pass over the river
As the tide turned in its sleep.

ELEANOR FARJEON

February 13

A Council of Mice

A council of mice on an argument nice,
How to outwit a cat, chose to call.
They assembled, and one his speech thus begun:
Mr Chairman and gentlemen all, list to me,
Mr Chairman and gentlemen all.

A plan I have pat, to escape from this cat,
Let her steal on us ever so sly.
To know when she comes and get safe to our homes –
A bell round her neck let us tie, don't you see?
A bell round her neck let us tie.

The plan they all chose, but an old mouse arose,
And said, like a very grave don:
The plan of the bell may do very well,
But gentlemen, who'll tie it on? Tell me that?
But gentlemen, who'll tie it on?

ANON E. MOUSE

43

February 14   St Valentine's Day

The Bargain

My true love hath my heart, and I have his,
　　By just exchange, one for the other given.
I hold his dear, and mine he cannot miss,
　　There never was a better bargain driven.
His heart in me keeps me and him in one,
　　My heart in him his thoughts and senses guides;
He loves my heart, for once it was his own,
　　I cherish his, because in me it bides.
His heart his wound received from my sight,
　　My heart was wounded with his wounded heart;
For as from me on him his hurt did light,
　　So still methought in me his hurt did smart.
　　　　Both equal hurt, in this change sought our bliss:
　　　　My true-love hath my heart, and I have his.

PHILIP SIDNEY

February 15

The Water is Wide

The water is wide, I cannot get o'er,
And neither have I wings to fly.
Give me a boat that will carry two,
And both shall row, my love and I.

Down in the meadows the other day,
A-gathering flowers both fine and gay,
A-gathering flowers both red and blue
I little thought what love can do.

I leaned my back up against some oak,
Thinking that he was a trusty tree,
But first he bended and then he broke
And so did my false love to me.

ANON

February 16

Beautiful Soup

Beautiful Soup, so rich and green,
    Waiting in a hot tureen!
Who for such dainties would not stoop?
Soup of the evening, beautiful Soup!
Soup of the evening, beautiful Soup!
    Beau-ootiful Soo-oop!
    Beau-ootiful Soo-oop!
Soo-oop of the e-e-evening,
    Beautiful, beautiful Soup!

Beautiful Soup! Who cares for fish,
    Game, or any other dish?
Who would not give all else for two p-
ennyworth only of beautiful Soup?
Pennyworth only of beautiful Soup?
    Beau-ootiful Soo-oop!
    Beau-ootiful Soo-oop!
    Soo-oop of the e-e-evening,
    Beautiful, beauti-FUL SOUP!

LEWIS CARROLL

February 17

Windy Nights

Whenever the moon and stars are set,
　　Whenever the wind is high,
All night long in the dark and wet,
　　A man goes riding by.
Late in the night when the fires are out,
Why does he gallop and gallop about?

Whenever the trees are crying aloud,
　　And ships are tossed at sea,
By, on the highway, low and loud,
　　By at the gallop goes he.
By at the gallop he goes, and then,
By he comes back at the gallop again.

ROBERT LOUIS STEVENSON

February 18

Picnic

Ella, fell a
Maple tree.
Hilda, build a
Fire for me.

Teresa, squeeze a
Lemon, so.
Amanda, hand a
Plate to Flo.

Nora, pour a
Cup of tea.
Fancy, Nancy,
What a spree!

HUGH LOFTING

February 19

One Misty Moisty Morning

One misty moisty morning
When cloudy was the weather,
There I met an old man
Clothed all in leather;
Clothed all in leather,
With cap under his chin –
How do you do and how do you do
And how do you do again?

ANON

February 20

Trees

The Oak is called the king of trees,
The Aspen quivers in the breeze,
The Poplar grows up straight and tall,
The Peach tree spreads along the wall,
The Sycamore gives pleasant shade,
The Willow droops in watery glade,
The Fir tree useful timber gives,
The Beech amid the forest lives.

SARA COLERIDGE

February 21

For Want of a Nail

For want of a nail
    The shoe was lost,
For want of a shoe,
    The horse was lost,
For want of the horse,
    The rider was lost,
For want of the rider,
    The battle was lost,
For want of the battle,
    The kingdom was lost –

All for the want
Of a horse-shoe nail.

ANON

February 22

Cock-Crow

Out of the wood of thoughts that grows by night
To be cut down by the sharp axe of light –
Out of the night, two cocks together crow,
Cleaving the darkness with a silver blow:
And bright before my eyes twin trumpeters stand,
Heralds of splendour, one at either hand,
Each facing each as in a coat of arms:
The milkers lace their boots up at the farms.

EDWARD THOMAS

February 23

Piggy on the Railway

Piggy on the railway
Picking up stones,
Along came an engine
And broke Piggy's bones.

'Oy' says Piggy,
'That's not fair.'
'Pooh,' says the engine-driver,
'I don't care.'

ANON

51

February 24

from The Jumblies

They went to sea in a Sieve, they did,
   In a Sieve they went to sea:
In spite of all their friends could say,
On a winter's morn, on a stormy day,
   In a Sieve they went to sea!
And when the Sieve turned round and round,
And every one cried, 'You'll all be drowned!'
They called aloud, 'Our Sieve ain't big,
But we don't care a button! we don't care a fig!
   In a Sieve we'll go to sea!'
     Far and few, far and few,
      Are the lands where the Jumblies live;
      Their heads are green, and their hands are blue,
      And they went to sea in a Sieve.

EDWARD LEAR

February 25

from Travels

I should like to rise and go
Where the golden apples grow;–
Where below another sky
Parrot islands anchored lie,
And, watched by cockatoos and goats,
Lonely Crusoes building boats;–
Where in sunshine reaching out
Eastern cities, miles about,
Are with mosque and minaret
Among sandy gardens set,
And the rich goods from near and far
Hang for sale in the bazaar.

ROBERT LOUIS STEVENSON

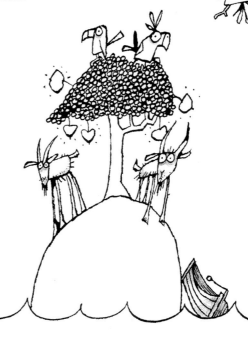

February 26

And God Said to the Little Boy

And God said to the little boy
As the little boy came out of chapel
Little boy, little boy, little boy
Did you eat that there apple?
And the little boy answered No, Lord.

And God said to the little girl
As the little girl came out of chapel
Little girl, little girl, little girl,
Did you eat that there apple?
And the little girl answered No, Lord.

Then the Lord pointed with his finger
And fixed them both with his stare,
And he said in a voice like a Rolls Royce
Well, what are them two cores doing there?

GEORGE BARKER

February 27

from The Song of Hiawatha

By the shore of Gitche Gumee,
By the shining Big-Sea-Water,
Stood the wigwam of Nokomis,
Daughter of the Moon, Nokomis.
Dark behind it rose the forest,
Rose the black and gloomy pine-trees,
Rose the firs with cones upon them;
Bright before it beat the water,
Beat the clear and sunny water,
Beat the shining Big-Sea-Water.

HENRY WADSWORTH LONGFELLOW

February 28

A Good Night Out (for the Dog)

There once was a man of Bengal,
Who was asked to a fancy dress ball;
   He murmured 'I'll risk it
   And go as a biscuit' –
But a dog ate him up in the hall.

ANON

February 29 Only to be read in a Leap Year

Gee Whizz! Gosh! Lummy! Coo! The Town Bully's Chased by a Kangaroo!

Headline in a Comic of the 1940s

IF TODAY IS YOUR BIRTHDAY AND ONLY IF SO YOU CAN READ THE REST OF THIS PAGE. I'D BETTER WHISPER – (because you only have a birthday once every four years, you are one-quarter the age of everybody else, in which case you are very very very very tall and wise for your age. So, in order that you shall become one of the wisest whizzes in the world, I have purchased a special bundle of Incredibly Rare Wisdom from Dame Grizzle Murkin and her cat Lurkin. You can read them in any order at all . . .)

*Early to bed and early to rise

Sharpens your teeth and narrows your eyes.

*A banana peeled is a banana eaten.

*Get your work done, and then have fun.

*The loudest music is played in clothes shops.

*If your dog cries in her sleep, tell her it's only a dream.

*Two computers aren't twice as clever.

*Don't play Sardines with a party of hippopotami.

*Your body knows it's wrong to run uphill.

*If you can't have fun with a tin of treacle, you can't have fun at all.

*It's a chilly clock if its hands need gloves.

*Never lend your bagpipes to a chimpanzee.

*Every Thursday longs to be Saturday.

*Say Hello if you meet a Ghost.

*Only Goldilocks was greedy enough to eat three bowls of porridge.

*We don't need lion-tamers,

We need man-tamers.

*What use are paper-clips if you're a Teddy Bear?

*It's no use phoning Queen Victoria.

*Look hard at the stars and see them wobble.

*Three grapes and an eel make a weird meal.

*Most mice prefer cheese to chess.

*If the world didn't have an Equator,

its trousers would fall down.

ADRIAN MYSTICAL

March 1

The Feast of Lanterns

Tching-a-ring-a-ring-tching,
Feast of Lanterns,
What a lot of chop-sticks, bombs and gongs:
Four-and-twenty thousand crink-um-crank-ums,
All among the bells and the ding-dongs.

ANON

March 2

from Incidents in the Life of My Uncle Arly

O my aged Uncle Arly!
Sitting on a heap of Barley
    Thro' the silent hours of night,–
Close beside a leafy thicket:–
On his nose there was a Cricket,–
In his hat a Railway-Ticket; –
    (But his shoes were far too tight.)

EDWARD LEAR

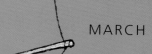

March 3

Ten Angels Alone on Trapezes

I saw ten angels alone on trapezes,
Nine monkeys dancing in fire,
I saw eight snowflakes falling in lakes
And seven fish caught on a wire.

I saw six pirates with sacks full of treasure,
Five tigers sharing a crust,
Four budgerigars playing guitars
And three blackthorns covered in dust.

I saw two shadows without any owners,
One faded and then was gone,
Its friend searched for it in the darkness,
And then, of course, there were none.

BRIAN PATTEN

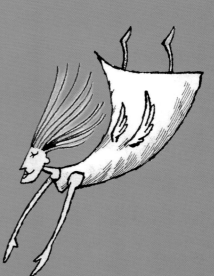

March 4

The Pasture

I'm going out to clean the pasture spring;
I'll only stop to rake the leaves away
(And wait to watch the water clear, I may):
I shan't be gone long. – You come too.

I'm going out to fetch the little calf
That's standing by the mother. It's so young
It totters when she licks it with her tongue.
I shan't be gone long. – You come too.

ROBERT FROST

March 5

A Farmer's Boy

They strolled down the lane together,
The sky was studded with stars –
They reached the gate in silence
And he lifted down the bars –
She neither smiled nor thanked him –
Because she knew not how;
For he was just a farmer's boy
And she was a Jersey Cow.

ANON

March 6

We like March: His Shoes are Purple –
He is new and high –
Makes he Mud for Dog and Peddler,
Makes he Forests dry.
Knows the Adder Tongue his coming
And presents her Spot –
Stands the Sun so close and mighty
That our Minds are hot.

News is he of all the others –
Bold it were to die
With the Blue Birds exercising
On his British Sky.

EMILY DICKINSON

March 7

The sausage is a cunning bird
With feathers long and wavy;
It swims about the frying pan
And makes its nest in gravy.

ANON

March 8

The Christening

What shall I call
     My dear little dormouse?
His eyes are small,
     But his tail is e-nor-mouse.

I sometimes call him Terrible John,
'Cos his tail goes on–
And on–
And on.
And I sometimes call him Terrible Jack,
'Cos his tail goes on to the end of his back.
And I sometimes call him Terrible James,
'Cos he says he likes me calling him names . . .

     But I think I shall call him Jim,
     'Cos I *am* so fond of him.

A. A. MILNE

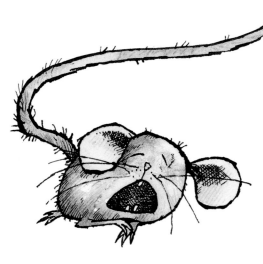

March 9

The Red Wheelbarrow

so much depends
upon

a red wheel
barrow

glazed with rain
water

beside the white
chickens.

WILLIAM CARLOS WILLIAMS

March 10

Hares at Play

The birds are gone to bed, the cows are still,
And sheep lie panting on each old mole-hill;
And underneath the willow's grey-green bough,
Like toil a-resting, lies the fallow plough.
The timid hares throw daylight fears away
On the lane's road to dust and dance and play,
Then dabble in the grain by naught deterred
To lick the dew-fall from the barley's beard;
Then out they sturt again and round the hill
Like happy thoughts dance, squat, and loiter still,
Till milking maidens in the early morn
Jingle their yokes and sturt them in the corn;
Through well-known beaten paths each nimbling hare
Sturts quick as fear, and seeks his hidden lair.

JOHN CLARE

(to sturt is to start or jump up)

March 11

from Tartary

If I were Lord of Tartary,
    Myself, and me alone,
My bed should be of ivory,
    Of beaten gold my throne;
And in my court should peacocks flaunt,
And in my forests tigers haunt,
And in my pools great fishes slant
    Their fins athwart the sun.

If I were Lord of Tartary,
    Trumpeters every day
To all my meals should summon me,
    And in my courtyards bray;
And in the evening lamps should shine,
Yellow as honey, red as wine,
While harp, and flute, and mandoline
    Made music sweet and gay.

WALTER DE LA MARE

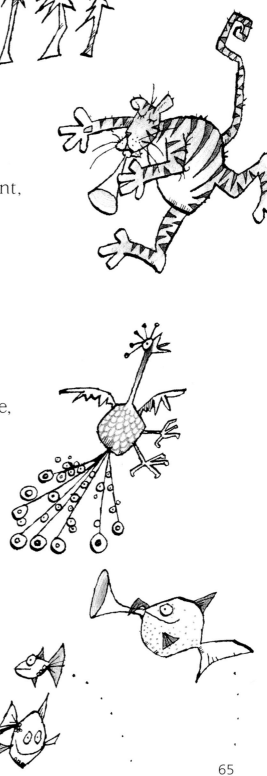

65

March 12

from The Quangle-Wangle's Hat

On top of the Crumpetty Tree
    The Quangle Wangle sat,
But his face you could not see,
    On account of his Beaver Hat.
For his Hat was a hundred and two feet wide,
    With ribbons and bibbons on every side
And bells, and buttons, and loops, and lace,
    So that nobody ever could see the face
        Of the Quangle Wangle Quee.

EDWARD LEAR

March 13

Hark, hark! the lark at heaven's gate sings,
    And Phoebus 'gins arise,
His steeds to water at those springs
    On chaliced flowers that lies;
And winking Mary-buds begin
    To ope their golden eyes.

WILLIAM SHAKESPEARE

March 14

from The School-Boy

I love to rise in a summer morn
When the birds sing on every tree;
The distant huntsman winds his horn,
And the sky-lark sings with me:
O, what sweet company!

But to go to school in a summer morn,
O! it drives all joy away;
Under a cruel eye outworn
The little ones spend the day
In sighing and dismay.

WILLIAM BLAKE

March 15

Thaw

Over the land freckled with snow half-thawed
The speculating rooks at their nests cawed
And saw from elm-tops, delicate as flowers of grass,
What we below could not see, Winter pass.

EDWARD THOMAS

March 16

Measles in the Ark

The night it was horribly dark,
The measles broke out in the Ark;
Little Japheth, and Shem, and all the young Hams,
Were screaming at once for potatoes and clams.
And 'What shall I do,' said poor Mrs Noah,
'All alone by myself in this terrible shower?
I know what I'll do: I'll step down in the hold,
And wake up a lioness grim and old,
And tie her close to the children's door,
And give her ginger-cake to roar
At the top of her voice for an hour or more;
And I'll tell the children to cease their din,
Or I'll let that grim old party in,
To stop their squeazles and likewise their measles.'
She practised this with the greatest success:
She was everyone's grandmother, I guess.

SUSAN COOLIDGE

March 17

from Ode

We are the music-makers,
    And we are the dreamers of dreams,
Wandering by lone sea-breakers,
    And sitting by desolate streams;
World-losers and world forsakers,
    On whom the pale moon gleams:
Yet we are the movers and shakers
    Of the world for ever, it seems.

ARTHUR O'SHAUGHNESSY

March 18

Humbydrum

As I went by Humbydrum,
By Humbydrum by Dreary,
I met Jehoky Poky
Carrying away Jaipeery.

If I had had my tip my tap,
My tip my tap my teerie,
I wouldn't have let Jehoky Poky
Carry away Jaipeery.

ANON

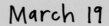

March 19

My Fairy

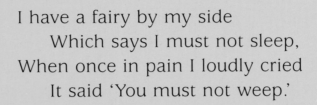

I have a fairy by my side
    Which says I must not sleep,
When once in pain I loudly cried
    It said 'You must not weep.'

If, full of mirth, I smile and grin,
    It says 'You must not laugh,'
When once I wished to drink some gin,
    It said 'You must not quaff.'

When once a meal I wished to taste
    It said 'You must not bite'.
When to the wars I went in haste,
    It said 'You must not fight.'

'What may I do?' At length I cried,
    Tired of the painful task,
The fairy quietly replied,
    And said 'You must not ask.'

    Moral: You mustn't.

ANON

March 20

The Cat's Serenade

The lamps are faintly gleaming, love,
The thief on walk is scheming, love!
　　And it's sweet to crawl
　　Over the dead wall,
While the tabbies are gently screaming, love!

Then put out one paw so white, my dear,
The house-tops are covered with light, my dear,
　　Through the day, at our ease,
　　We'll sleep when we please,
But we'll ramble abroad through the night, my dear.

ANON

March 21

The Dog and the Sausage

A doggie stole a sausage
When he was underfed.
The butcher saw him take it
And now poor doggie's dead.

And all the little doggies
They gathered there that night.
They built a little tombstone
And on it they did write:

"A doggie stole a sausage
When he was underfed.
The butcher saw him take it
And now poor doggie's dead.

And all the little doggies . . ."

ANON

March 22

from The Fairies

Up the airy mountain,
　　Down the rushy glen,
We daren't go a-hunting
　　For fear of little men;
Wee folk, good folk,
　　Trooping all together;
Green jacket, red cap,
　　And white owl's feather!

Down along the rocky shore
　　Some make their home,
They live on crispy pancakes
　　Of yellow tide-foam;
Some in the reeds
　　Of the black mountain-lake,
With frogs for their watchdogs,
　　All night awake.

WILLIAM ALLINGHAM

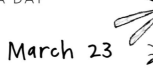

March 23

from The Butterfly's Ball

Come, take up your hats, and away let us haste
To the Butterfly's Ball and the Grasshopper's Feast.
The Trumpeter Gadfly has summoned the Crew
And the Revels are now only waiting for you.

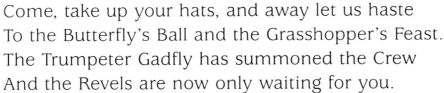

Along came the Gnat and the Dragon-Fly too,
With all their Relations, Green, Orange and Blue.
And there came the Moth with his plumage of down
And the Hornet, in Jacket of Yellow and Brown
Who with him the Wasp, his Companion, did bring,
But they promised that Evening to lay down their Sting.

And the sly little Dormouse crept out of his hole
And brought to the feast his blind Brother the Mole.
A Mushroom their Table, and on it was laid
A Water-dock Leaf, which a Table-cloth made.
Then as Evening gave way to the Shadows of Night,
Their Watchman, the Glow-worm, came out with a light.

ANON

March 24

The Canary

Mary had a little bird
    With feathers bright and yellow,
Slender legs – upon my word
    He was a handsome fellow!

Sweetest notes he always sung,
    Which much delighted Mary;
Often where his cage was hung
    She sat to hear Canary.

Crumbs of bread and dainty seeds
    She carried to him daily;
Seeking for the early weeds,
    She decked his palace gaily.

ANON

March 25

Cock Robin

Who killed Cock Robin?
    I, said the Sparrow,
    With my bow and arrow,
I killed Cock Robin.

Who saw him die?
    I, said the Fly,
    With my little eye,
I saw him die.

Who'll dig his grave?
    I, said the Owl,
    With my spade and trowel,
I'll dig his grave.

All the birds of the air fell a-sighing and a-sobbing
When they heard of the death of poor Cock Robin.

ANON

March 26

The Johnsons Had a Baby

The Johnsons had a baby,
They called him Tiny Tim, Tim, Tim,
They put him in a bath tub
To see if he could swim, swim, swim.
He drank a bowl of water
And ate a bar of soap, soap, soap,
He tried to eat the bath tub
But it wouldn't fit down his throat, throat, throat.
Mummy, Mummy, I feel ill,
Call the Doctor down the hill.
In came the Doctor, in came the Nurse,
In came the Lady with the Alligator Purse.
'Doctor, Doctor, will I die?'
'Yes, my son but do not cry –
Close your eyes and count to ten.'
'One, two, three, four, five, six, seven, eight, nine, ten.'
Out went the Doctor, out went the Nurse,
Out went the Lady with the Alligator Purse.

ANON

March 27

The Excellent Choice of Elizabeth Botter

Betty Botter bought some butter,
But, she said, the butter's bitter;
If I put it in my batter
It will make my batter bitter,
But a bit of better butter
That will make my batter better.
So she bought a bit of butter
Better than her bitter butter,
And she put it in her batter
And the batter was not bitter.
So 'twas better Betty Botter bought a bit of better butter.

ANON

March 28

The Scottish Mermaids

Four-and-twenty Mermaids,
They left the port of Leith
To tempt the fine old Hermit
Who dwelt upon Inchkeith.

No boat, nor waft, nor crayer,
Nor craft had they, nor oars nor sails;
Their lily hands were oars enough,
Their tillers were their tails.

ANON

March 29

O wind, where have you been,
    That you blow so sweet?
Among the violets
    Which blossom at your feet.

The honeysuckle waits
    For summer and the heat.
But violets in the chilly Spring
    Make the turf so sweet.

CHRISTINA ROSSETTI

March 30

When that I was and a little tiny boy,
    With hey, ho, the wind and the rain,
A foolish thing was but a toy,
    For the rain it raineth every day.

But when I came to man's estate,
    With hey, ho, the wind and the rain,
'Gainst knaves and thieves men shut their gate,
    For the rain it raineth every day.

But when I came, alas! to wive,
    With hey, ho, the wind and the rain,
By swaggering could I never thrive,
    For the rain it raineth every day.

But when I came unto my beds,
    With hey, ho, the wind and the rain,
With toss-pots still had drunken heads,
    For the rain it raineth every day.

A great while ago the world begun,
    With hey, ho, the wind and the rain,
But that's all one, our play is done,
    And we'll strive to please you every day.

WILLIAM SHAKESPEARE, FROM *TWELFTH NIGHT*

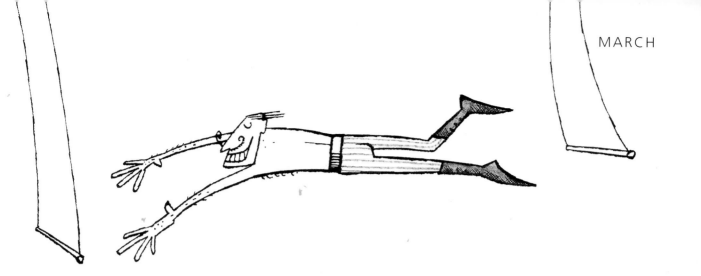

March 31

The Man on the Flying Trapeze

Oh, the girl that I loved she was handsome,
I tried all I knew her to please,
But I couldn't please her a quarter as well
As the man on the flying trapeze.

Oh, he flies through the air with the greatest of ease,
This daring young man on the flying trapeze.
His figure is handsome, all girls he can please,
And my true love he stole her away.

My love packed her bags and eloped in the night,
To go-o with him at his ease.
He lowered her down from a four-storey flight,
By means of his flying trapeze.

Oh, he flies through the air with the greatest of ease . . .

ANON

April 1

The Greatest Poem in the World

This is the first line of the Greatest Poem in History
And this is the second great line of the work.
Down on your knees! As this Poetic Mystery
Lumbers toward you like a Monster out of the murk.

Lo! how the Heavens applaud it with blunderbusses,
Granting this Poem a Royal Salute,
Musical angels arriving in thunderbusses
Raise up their trumpets to rooty-toot-toot –

That is as much of the Poem
as we print here,
It's far too Mighty to fit on this page,
So I will leave you,
but first let me hint here –
This will be the
Most Famous Poem of the Age.

ADRIAN MITCHELL (SHADOW POET LAUREATE)

URGENT MESSAGE

A duck in the pond,
A fish in the pool,
Whoever reads this
Is a big April Fool!

ANON

April 2

A Farm Picture

Through the ample open door of the peaceful country barn,
A sunlit pasture field, with cattle and horses feeding;
And haze, and vista, and the far horizon, fading away.

WALT WHITMAN

April 3

If you can walk
You can dance
If you can talk
You can sing

ANON

April 4

The Tyger

Tyger! Tyger! burning bright
In the forests of the night,
What immortal hand or eye
Could frame thy fearful symmetry?

In what distant deeps or skies
Burnt the fire of thine eyes?
On what wings dare he aspire?
What the hand, dare seize the fire?

And what shoulder, & what art,
Could twist the sinews of thy heart?
And when thy heart began to beat,
What dread hand? & what dread feet?

What the hammer? what the chain?
In what furnace was thy brain?
What the anvil? what dread grasp
Dare its deadly terrors clasp?

When the stars threw down their spears,
And water'd heaven with their tears,
Did he smile his work to see?
Did he who made the Lamb make thee?

Tyger! Tyger! burning bright
In the forests of the night,
What immortal hand or eye
Dare frame thy fearful symmetry?

WILLIAM BLAKE

April 5

The Postman's Belle

Miss Penelope Birch lived near Islington church,
And after her lovers a host ran,
Till the choice of this Belle on a General fell,
One Wilkins, the General Postman.

As each morn he passed by, how she'd ogle and sigh
And quick from her coffee and toast ran;
Or if e'er sparks at night in her candle shone bright,
That meant letters from Wilkins the Postman.

Soon a loud double knock to her nerves gave a shock,
She trembled, and pale as a ghost ran;
The next letter you bring, please to come with a Ring.
So he did – and she married her Postman.

ANON

April 6

The Lamb

Little Lamb, who made thee?
Dost thou know who made thee?
Gave thee life & bid thee feed,
By the stream & o'er the mead;
Gave thee clothing of delight,
Softest clothing wooly bright;
Gave thee such a tender voice,
Making all the vales rejoice!
Little Lamb who made thee?
Dost thou know who made thee?

Little Lamb I'll tell thee,
Little Lamb I'll tell thee!
He is called by thy name,
For he calls himself a Lamb:
He is meek & he is mild,
He became a little child:
I a child & thou a lamb,
We are called by his name.
Little Lamb God bless thee.
Little Lamb God bless thee.

WILLIAM BLAKE

April 7

Who'll Buy Primroses?

Come buy from poor Mary, primroses I sell,
Through London's famed city I'm known mighty well;
Though my heart is quite sunk, yet I constantly cry:
Come, who'll buy primroses? Come, who'll buy primroses?
    Who'll buy? Who'll buy?

My companions despise me, and say I am proud
Because I avoid them and keep from their crowd;
From wicked temptations I ever will fly,
I live by primroses, come, who'll buy primroses?
    Who'll buy? Who'll buy?

ANON

April 8

The Hare

In the black furrow of a field
I saw an old witch-hare this night;
And she cocked a lissome ear,
And she eyed the moon so bright,
And she nibbled of the green;
And I whispered 'Whsst! witch-hare,'
Away like a ghostie o'er the field
She fled, and left the moonlight there.

WALTER DE LA MARE

April 9

The I-Got-'Em-Man

I got yellow mangoes! I got catfish!
I got buffaloes! I got 'em!

I got stringbeans! I got cabbages!
I got collard greens! I got 'em!

I got honeydews! I got cantaloupes!
I got watermelons! I got 'em!

I got fishes! I got fruits!
I got vegetables – yes, indeed!
I got any kind of vittles at all,
Anything at all you need!

I'm the I-Got-Em Man!

AMERICAN STREET-SELLER'S CRY

April 10

from The First Swallow

The gorse is yellow on the heath;
    The banks with speed-well flowers are gay;
The oaks are budding, and beneath,
    The hawthorn soon will bear the wreath,
The silver wreath of May.

The welcomed guest of settled spring,
The swallow, too, is come at last.

CHARLOTTE SMITH

April 11

In the Spring a fuller crimson comes upon the robin's breast;
In the Spring the wanton lapwing gets himself another crest;

In the Spring a livelier iris changes on the burnish'd dove;
In the Spring a young man's fancy lightly turns to thoughts
    of love.

ALFRED TENNYSON

April 12

Come Out to Play

Girls and boys, come out to play,
The moon is shining as bright as day;
Leave your supper and leave your sleep
And join your playfellows in the street.
Come with a whoop, come with a call,
Come with a good will or not at all.
Up the ladder and down the wall,
A halfpenny bun shall serve us all.
You find milk and I'll find flour,
And we'll have a pudding in half an hour.

ANON

April 13

When the Movie Stood Still

I went to the pictures tomorrow
And took a front seat at the back.
I said to the lady behind me,
I cannot see over your hat.
She gave me some well-broken biscuits,
I ate them and gave her them back.
I fell from the pit to the gallery
And broke a front bone in my back.

ANON

April 14

Chorus

Ba-ba, black wool,
  Have you any sheep?
Yes, sir, a pack-ful,
  Creep, mouse, creep!
Four-and-twenty little maids
  Hanging out the pie,
Out jumped the honey-pot,
  Guy Fawkes, Guy!
Cross-latch, cross-latch,
  Sit and spin by the fire,
When the pie was opened,
  The bird was on the brier!

WILLIAM BRIGHTY RANDS

April 15

from To The Small Celandine

Pansies, lilies, kingcups, daisies,
Let them live upon their praises;
    Long as there's a sun that sets,
Primroses will have their glory;
    Long as there are violets,
They will have a place in story:
There's a flower that shall be mine,
'Tis the little Celandine.

WILLIAM WORDSWORTH

April 16

Where innocent bright-eyed daisies are,
    With blades of grass between,
Each daisy stands up like a star
    Out of a sky of green.

CHRISTINA ROSSETTI

April 17

Early Nightingale

When first we hear the shy-come nightingales,
They seem to mutter o'er their songs in fear,
And, climb we e'er so soft the spinney rails,
All stops as if no bird was anywhere.
The kindled bushes with the young leaves thin
Let curious eyes to search a long way in,
Until impatience cannot see or hear
The hidden music; gets but little way
Upon the path – when up the songs begin,
Full loud a moment and then low again.
But when a day or two confirms her stay
Boldly she sings and loud for half the day;
And soon the village brings the woodman's tale
Of having heard the new-come nightingale.

JOHN CLARE

April 18

Fantails

Up on the roof the Fantail Pigeons dream
Of dollops of curled cream.

At every morning window their soft voices
Comfort all the bedrooms with caresses.

'Peace, peace, peace,' through the day
The Fantails hum and murmur and pray.

Like a dream, where resting angels crowded
The roof-slope, that has not quite faded.

When they clatter up, and veer, and soar in a ring
It's as if the house suddenly sang something.

The cats of the house, purring on lap and knee,
Dig their claws and scowl with jealousy.

TED HUGHES

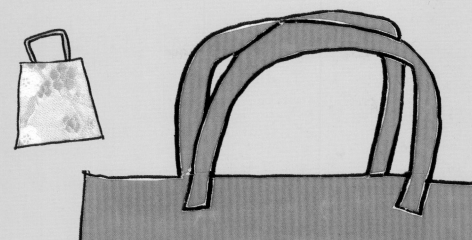

April 19

I've Been Shopping

I've been shopping – I've been shopping
To John Brown's in Regent Street,
And I'm hopping – and I'm hopping
With his shoes upon my feet.

I've been roaming – I've been roaming
For rose oil and lily rare,
And I'm coming – and I'm coming
With a bottle for my hair.

I've been roaming – I've been roaming
Up Bond Street and down Park Lane,
And I'm coming – and I'm coming
To my own house broke again.

ANON

April 20

My Pony

I had a little pony,
I called him Dapple Grey;
I lent him to a lady
To ride a mile away.

She whipped him, she lashed him,
She drove him through the mire.
I would not lend my pony now
For all the lady's hire.

ANON

April 21

Mule

My Mammy was a wall-eyed goat,
My Old Man was an ass,
And I feed myself off leather boots
And dynamite and grass;
For I'm a mule, a long-eared fool
And I ain't never been to school –
    Mammeee! Ma-ha-mam-hee!
    Heee-haw! Mamaah!
    Ma-ha-mee!

ANON

April 22

To Horse and Away!

To horse, my merry companions all,
To horse, to horse and away!
The sunbeams on the mountains fall,
The wood-lark sings, the falconers call,
    And hail the dawning day.

The generous steed, so plump and fair,
Impatient snuffs the morning air,
    To horse, to horse and away!
Already her game the falcon spies,
In vain the prey to escape her tries,
Already she seems to reach the skies!
    To horse, to horse and away!

THOMAS DIBDIN

April 23

We Be Three Poor Fishermen
(to be sung as a round)

We be three poor fishermen,
Who daily trawl the seas;
We spend our lives in jeopardy
While others live at ease.

The sky looks black around, around, around,
The sky looks black around.
And he that would be merry, boys,
Come haul his boat aground.

We cast our lines along the shore
In stormy wind or rain;
And every night we land our nets
Till daylight comes again.

The sky looks black around, around, around . . .

ANON

April 24

Gratitude

I found a starving cat in the street:
    It cried for food and a place by the fire.
I carried it home, and I strove to meet
    The claims of its desire.

And since its desire was a little fish,
    A little hay and a little milk.
I gave it cream in a silver dish
    And a basket lined with silk.

And when we came to the grateful pause
    When it should have fawned on the hand that fed,
It turned to a devil all teeth and claws,
    Scratched me and bit me and fled.

To pay for the fish and the milk and the hay
    With a purr had been an easy task:
But its hate and my blood were required to pay
    For the gifts that it did not ask.

E. NESBIT

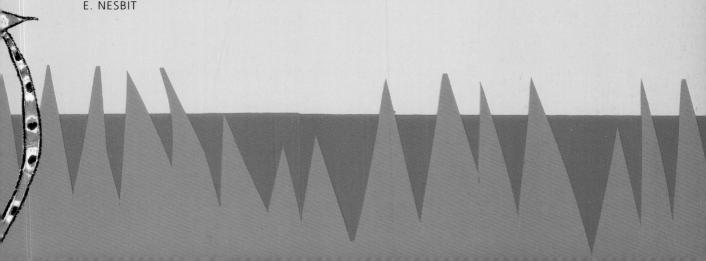

April 25

Caliban Reassures Castaways on Prospero's Island

Be not afeard: the isle is full of noises,
Sounds and sweet airs, that give delight, and hurt not.
Sometimes a thousand twangling instruments
Will hum about mine ears, and sometimes voices
That if I then had waked after long sleep
Will make me sleep again; and then in dreaming,
The clouds methought would open and show riches
Ready to drop upon me; that, when I waked
I cried to dream again.

WILLIAM SHAKESPEARE, FROM *THE TEMPEST*

April 26

Song

It was a lover and his lass
With a hey and a ho and a hey-nonino!
That o'er the green cornfield did pass
In the spring time, the only pretty ring-time,
When birds do sing hey ding a ding;
Sweet lovers love the Spring.

WILLIAM SHAKESPEARE

April 27
Lullaby

Hush little baby, don't say a word,
Papa's going to buy you a mocking bird.

And if that mocking bird won't sing,
Papa's going to buy you a diamond ring.

Now if that diamond ring turns to brass,
Papa's going to buy you a looking-glass.

And if that looking-glass gets broke,
Papa's going to buy you a billy-goat.

And if that billy-goat runs wild,
You're still Papa's special child.

So hush little baby, don't say a word,
Papa's going to buy you a mocking bird.

ANON

April 28

How Doth . . .

How doth the little crocodile
    Improve his shining tail,
And pour the waters of the Nile
    On every golden scale!

How cheerfully he seems to grin,
    How neatly spreads his claws,
And welcomes little fishes in
    With gently smiling jaws!

LEWIS CARROLL

April 29

The Cuckoo in Scotland

The cuckoo's a bonnie bird,
He sings as he flies;
He brings us good tidings,
He tells us nae lies.

He drinks the cold water
To keep his voice clear;
And he'll come again
In the spring of the year.

ANON

April 30

Under the greenwood tree
Who loves to lie with me
And tune his merry note
Unto the sweet bird's throat –
Come hither, come hither, come hither!
Here shall we see
No enemy
But winter and rough weather.

WILLIAM SHAKESPEARE

May 1

May the First

The fair maid who, the first of May,
Goes to the fields at break of day
And washes in dew from the hawthorn tree,
Will ever after handsome be.

ANON

May 2

Now the bright morning star, day's harbinger,
Comes dancing from the East, and leads with her
The flowery May, who from her green lap throws
The yellow cowslip and the pale primrose.
    Hail, bounteous May! that doth inspire
    Mirth, and youth, and warm desire.

JOHN MILTON

May 3

Night Song of the Fish

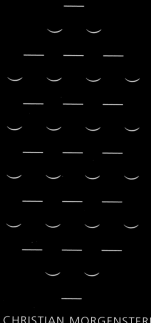

CHRISTIAN MORGENSTERN

May 4

The Mad Hatter's Song

Twinkle, twinkle, little bat!
How I wonder what you're at!
Up above the world you fly,
Like a tea-tray in the sky.

LEWIS CARROLL

105

May 5

The English Game

Of all the great games ever practised or known
Cricket stands tall in a class of its own
And wherever the leather by willow is smitten
The Cricketing nation all fear is Great Britain!

So bash me a boundary, catch me a catch,
I wager we'll triumph in every match.
So bowl me a bouncer and whack down that wicket
And show the whole world how old England plays Cricket.

Those Springboks and Kiwis are all doomed to failure,
And so are the big-talking boys from Australia,
Sri Lanka surrenders, the Windies get windier
As Pakistan topples and under goes India.

So bash me a boundary, catch me a catch . . .

ADRIAN MITCHELL

May 6

When daisies pied and violets blue
    And lady smocks all silver-white
And cuckoo buds of yellow hue
    Do paint the meadows with delight,
The cuckoo then, on every tree,
    Sings cuckoo, cuckoo.

WILLIAM SHAKESPEARE

May 7

There once were three owls in a wood
Who always sang hymns when they could.
    What the words were about
    One could never make out,
But one felt it was doing them good.

ANON

May 8

from The Pied Piper

Into the street the Piper stept,
    Smiling first a little smile,
As if he knew what magic slept
    In his quiet pipe the while;
Then, like a musical adept,
To blow the pipe his lips he wrinkled,
And green and blue his sharp eyes twinkled,
Like a candle-flame where salt is sprinkled;
And ere three shrill notes the pipe uttered,
You heard as if an army muttered;
And the muttering grew to a grumbling;
And the grumbling grew to a mighty rumbling;
And out of the houses the rats came tumbling.

Great rats, small rats, lean rats, brawny rats,
Brown rats, black rats, grey rats, tawny rats,
Grave old plodders, gay young friskers,
    Fathers, mothers, uncles, cousins,
Cocking tails and pricking whiskers,
    Families by tens and dozens,
Brothers, sisters, husbands, wives -
Followed the Piper for their lives.
From street to street he piped advancing,
And step by step they followed dancing,
Until they came to the river Weser,
    Wherein all plunged and perished!

ROBERT BROWNING

May 9

Ophelia, in her Madness, Giving Flowers

There's rosemary, that's for remembrance, pray, love, remember:
and there is pansies, that's for thoughts . . .

There's fennel for you, and columbines; there's rue for you;
and here's some for me; we may call it herb o' grace o' Sundays.
O! you must wear your rue with a difference. There's a daisy;
I would give you some violets, but they withered all when my
father died. They say he made a good end. For bonny sweet
Robin is all my joy.

WILLIAM SHAKESPEARE, FROM *HAMLET*

May 10

The Sick Rose

O Rose thou art sick.
The invisible worm
That flies in the night
In the howling storm,

Has found out thy bed
Of crimson joy:
And his dark secret love
Does thy life destroy.

WILLIAM BLAKE

May 11

The Common Cormorant

The common cormorant or shag
Lays eggs inside a paper bag
The reason you will see no doubt
It is to keep the lightning out.
But what these unobservant birds
Have never noticed is that herds
Of wandering bears may come with buns
And steal the bags to hold the crumbs.

CHRISTOPHER ISHERWOOD

May 12

Early Space Travel

There was an old woman tossed up in a basket
    Nineteen times as high as the moon;
Where she was going I couldn't but ask it,
    For in her hand she carried a broom.

Old woman, old woman, old woman, quoth I,
    O whither, O whither, O whither so high,
To brush the cobwebs off the sky!
    Shall I go with thee? Aye, by and by.

ANON

May 13

Nottamun Town

In Nottamun Town not a soul would look up,
Not a soul would look up, not a soul would look down,
Not a soul would look up, not a soul would look down,
To tell me the way to Nottamun Town.

I rode a big horse that was called a grey mare,
Grey mane and tail, grey stripes down his back,
Grey mane and tail, grey stripes down his back,
There weren't a hair on him but what was called black.

Met the King and the Queen and a company of men
A-walking behind and a-riding before.
A stark naked drummer came walking along
With his hands in his bosom a-beating his drum.

ANON

May 14

from The Owl and the Pussy-cat

The Owl and the Pussy-cat went to sea
   In a beautiful pea-green boat,
They took some honey, and plenty of money,
   Wrapped up in a five-pound note.
The Owl looked up to the stars above,
   And sang to a small guitar,
'O lovely Pussy! O Pussy, my love
   What a beautiful Pussy you are,
     You are,
     You are!
   What a beautiful Pussy you are!'

Pussy said to the Owl, 'You elegant fowl!
   How charmingly sweet you sing!
O let us be married! too long we have tarried:
   But what shall we do for a ring?'
They sailed away, for a year and a day,
   To the land where the Bong-tree grows,
And there in a wood a Piggy-wig stood
   With a ring at the end of his nose,
     His nose,
     His nose,
   With a ring at the end of his nose.

EDWARD LEAR

May 15

from The Children of the Owl and the Pussy-cat

Our mother was the Pussy-cat, our father was the Owl,
And so we're partly little beasts and partly little fowl,
The brothers of our family have feathers and they hoot,
While all the sisters dress in fur and have long tails to boot.
 We all believe that little mice,
 For food are singularly nice.
Our mother died long years ago. She was a lovely cat
Her tail was 5 feet long, and grey with stripes, but what of that?
In Sila forest on the East of far Calabria's shore
She tumbled from a lofty tree – none ever saw her more.
Our owly father long was ill from sorrow and surprise,
But with the feathers of his tail he wiped his weeping eyes.
And in the hollow of a tree in Sila's inmost maze
We made a happy home and there we pass our obvious days.

EDWARD LEAR

May 16

Salt, Mustard, Vinegar, Pepper

Salt, Mustard, Vinegar, Pepper,
French Almond Rock,
Bread and butter for your supper
That's all mother's got.
Eggs and bacon, salted herring,
Put them in a pot,
Pickled onions, apple pudding –
We will eat the lot.

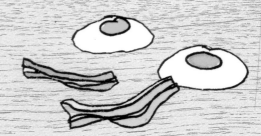

Salt, Mustard, Vinegar, Pepper,
Pig's head and trout,
Bread and butter for your supper
O U T spells out!

ANON

May 17

The Hiccup Fairy

'Twas the Hiccup Fairy,
That hiccetycupping blonde,
'Twas the Hiccup Fairy
Touched me (hiccup!) with her wand.
So for every hiccup
I gave her a kick up –
She landed in Belchy Pond.

ADRIAN MITCHELL

May 18

from The Spider and the Fly

'Will you walk into my parlour?' said the Spider to the Fly,
'Tis the prettiest little parlour that ever you did spy;
The way into my parlour is up a winding stair,
And I have many curious things to show when you are there.'
'Oh no, no,' said the little Fly, 'to ask me is in vain,
For who goes up your winding stair can ne'er come down again.'

MARY HOWITT

May 19

The All-Weather Hiawatha

When he killed the Mudjokivis,
Of the skin he made him mittens,
Made them with the fur side inside,
Made them with the skin side outside.
He, to get the warm side inside,
Put the inside skin side outside;
He, to get the cold side outside,
Put the warm side fur side inside.
That's why he put fur side inside,
Why he put the skin side outside,
Why he turned them inside outside.

ANON

May 20

a cat, a horse and the sun

a cat mistrusts the sun
keeps out of its way
only where sun and shadow meet
it moves

a horse loves the sun
it basks all day
snorts
and beats its hooves

the sun likes horses
but hates cats
that is why it makes hay
and heats tin roofs

ROGER MCGOUGH

May 21

Child on Top of a Greenhouse

The wind billowing out the seat of my britches,
My feet crackling splinters of glass and dried putty,
The half-grown chrysanthemums staring up like accusers,
Up through the streaked glass, flashing with sunlight,
A few white clouds all rushing eastward,
A line of elms plunging and tossing like horses,
And everyone, everyone pointing up and shouting!

THEODORE ROETHKE

May 22

from A Boy's Song

Where the pools are bright and deep,
Where the grey trout lies asleep,
Up the river and over the lea,
That's the way for Billy and me.

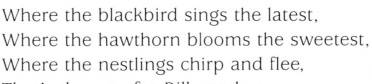

Where the blackbird sings the latest,
Where the hawthorn blooms the sweetest,
Where the nestlings chirp and flee,
That's the way for Billy and me.

JAMES HOGG

May 23

Tom the Piper

Tom, Tom, the Piper's son,
He learned to play when he was young,
But all the tune that he could play
Was Over the Hills and Far Away.

Now Tom, Tom learned to play with such skill
That whoever heard him could never keep still.
As soon as he played they began to dance,
Even Pigs on their hind legs would after him prance.

As Dolly was milking her Cow one day,
Tom took out his pipe and began to play
And Doll and her Cow danced the Cheshire Round
Till the pail of milk was knocked to the ground.

The Goat was a-going to shave off his beard,
But he soon stopped when Tom's music he heard,
He ran out of dance in a kind of a passion
And danced a fine dance which became all the fashion!

ANON

May 24

Where Go the Boats?

Dark brown is the river,
    Golden is the sand.
It flows along for ever,
    With trees on either hand.

Green leaves a-floating,
    Castles of the foam,
Boats of mine a-boating –
    Where will all come home?

On goes the river,
    And out past the mill,
Away down the valley,
    Away down the hill.

Away down the river,
    A hundred miles or more,
Other little children
    Shall bring my boats ashore.

ROBERT LOUIS STEVENSON

119

May 25

Turmut Hoeing

'Twas on a jolly summer's morn, the twenty-fifth of May,
Giles Croggins took his turmut-hoe, with which he
    trudged away;
For some delights in haymaking, and some they
    fancies mowin',
But of all the trades as I likes best, give I the turmut-hoein';
    For the fly, the fly, the fly is on the turmut;
    And it's all my eye for we to try, to keep fly off the turmut.

Now the first place as I went to work, it were at
    Farmer Tower's,
He vowed and sweared and then declared, I were a
    first rate hoer.
Now the next place as I went to work I took it by the job,
But if I'd ha' knowed it a little afore, I'd sooner been in quod.

When I was over at yonder farm, they sent for I a-mowin',
But I sent back word I'd sooner have the sack, than lose my
    turmut hoein',
Now all you jolly farming lads as bides at home so warm,
I now concludes my ditty with wishing you no harm.
    For the fly, the fly, the fly is on the turmut;
    And it's all my eye for we to try, to keep fly off the turmut.

ANON

May 26

Mrs Jaypher found a wafer
Which she stuck upon a note;
This she took and gave the cook.
Then she went and bought a boat
Which she paddled down the stream
Shouting, 'Ice produces cream,
Beer when churned produces butter!
Henceforth all the words I utter
Distant ages thus shall note –
"From the Jaypher Wisdom-Boat".'

EDWARD LEAR

May 27

Mrs Jaypher said it's safer
If you've lemons in your head
First to eat a pound of meat
And then to go at once to bed.

EDWARD LEAR

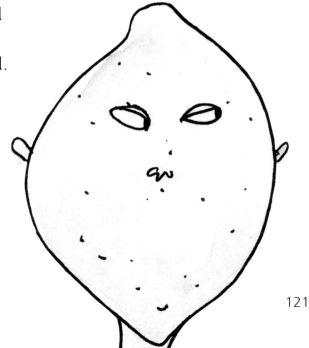

May 28

The Sleepy Giant

My age is three hundred and seventy-two.
And I think, with the deepest regret,
How I used to pick up and voraciously chew
The dear little boys whom I met.
I've eaten them raw, in their holiday suits;
I've eaten them curried with rice;
I've eaten them baked, in their jackets and boots.
And found them exceedingly nice.

But now that my jaws are too weak for such fare,
I think it exceedingly rude
To do such a thing, when I'm quite well aware
Little boys do not like to be chewed.

And so I contentedly live upon eels,
And try to do nothing amiss,
And I pass all the time I can spare from my meals
In innocent slumber – like this.

CHARLES E. CARRYL

May 29

Sergeant Brown's Parrot

Many policemen wear upon their shoulders
Cunning little radios. To pass away the time
They talk about the traffic to them, listen to the news,
And it helps them to Keep Down Crime.

But Sergeant Brown, he wears upon his shoulder
A tall green parrot as he's walking up and down
And all the parrot says is "Who's-a-pretty-boy-then?"
"I am," says Sergeant Brown.

KIT WRIGHT

May 30

Mrs Harding's Poem

"Parding, Mrs Harding,
Is my kitting in your kitching garding,
Gnawing of a mutting-bone?"

"No, he's gone to Londing."

"How many miles to Londing?
Eleving? I thought it was only seving.
Heavings! what a long way from home!"

ANON

May 31

from Block City

What are you able to build with your blocks?
Castles and palaces, temples and docks.
Rain may keep raining, and others go roam,
But I can be happy and building at home.

Let the sofa be mountains, the carpet be sea,
There I'll establish a city for me:
A kirk and a mill and a palace beside,
And a harbour as well where my vessels may ride.

Great is the palace with pillar and wall,
A sort of a tower on the top of it all,
And steps coming down in an orderly way
To where my toy vessels lie safe in the bay.

This one is sailing and that one is moored:
Hark to the song of the sailors on board!
And see on the steps of my palace, the kings
Coming and going with presents and things!

ROBERT LOUIS STEVENSON

124

May 35

* Baron Munchausen – the greatest liar in the world was born on this day, which was invented by Erich Kastner, author of *Emil and the Detectives* and *The 35th of May*.

PLEASE WRITE MORE VERSES FOR THIS SONG

It's the Thirty-Fifth of May
So throw your brains away
 Follow your nose
 Follow the Fleet
 Follow the Man
 With Hairy Feet
It's a doubly bubbly Holiday
It's the Thirty-Fifth of May

BARON MUNCHAUSEN
(AS DICTATED TO HIS HUMBLE SECRETARY ADRIAN MITCHELL)

June 1

Cargoes

Quinquireme of Nineveh from distant Ophir
Rowing home to haven in sunny Palestine,
With a cargo of ivory,
And apes and peacocks,
Sandalwood, cedarwood, and sweet white wine.

Stately Spanish galleon coming from the Isthmus,
Dipping through the Tropics by the palm-green shores,
With a cargo of diamonds,
Emeralds, amethysts,
Topazes, and cinnamon, and gold moidores.

Dirty British coaster with a salt-caked smoke stack
Butting through the Channel in the mad March days,
With a cargo of Tyne coal,
Road-rails, pig-lead,
Firewood, iron-ware, and cheap tin trays.

JOHN MASEFIELD

June 2

The Ship at Anchor

The sail clings lazily down the mast
    And our good ship sleeps on the tide,
Like the sea-bird that floats on the dark wave past
    With his broad wing closed to his side.
Then give way, lads, give way, stretch out the oar,
    Through the sparkling brine give way,
And to gentle hearts and bright eyes on shore,
    Sweet rest till return of day.

ANON

June 3

The Caterpillar

Brown and furry
Caterpillar in a hurry,
Take your walk
To the shady leaf, or stalk,
Or what not,
Which may be the chosen spot.
No toad spy you,
Hovering bird of prey pass by you;
Spin and die,
To live again a butterfly.

CHRISTINA ROSSETTI

June 4

To a Poor Old Woman

munching a plum on
the street a paper bag
of them in her hand

They taste good to her
They taste good
to her. They taste
good to her

You can see it by
the way she gives herself
to the one half
sucked out in her hand

Comforted
a solace of ripe plums
seeming to fill the air
They taste good to her

WILLIAM CARLOS WILLIAMS

June 5

King Arthur

When Good King Arthur ruled the land,
He was a goodly king;
He stole three pecks of barley-meal,
To make a bag-pudding.

A bag-pudding the Queen did make,
And stuffed it full of plums,
And in it put great lumps of fat,
As big as my two thumbs.

The King and Queen sat down to dine,
And all the court beside;
And what they could not eat that night,
The Queen next morning fried.

ANON

June 6

The Frog

What a wonderful bird the frog are –
When he sit, he stand almost.
When he hop, he fly almost.
He ain't got no sense hardly.
He ain't got no tail hardly either.
When he sit, he sit on what he ain't got –
almost.

ANON

June 7

I Had a Boat

I had a boat, and the boat had wings;
    And I did dream that we went a flying
Over the heads of queens and kings,
    Over the souls of dead and dying,
Up among the stars and the great white rings,
    And where the Moon on her back is lying.

MARY COLERIDGE

130

June 8

A Letter to Evelyn Baring

Thrippsy pillivinx,
    Inky tinky pobbleboskle abblesquabs? –
Flosky! beebul trimble flosky! – Okul
scratchabibblebongibo, viddle squibble tog-a-tog,
ferrymoyassity amsky flamsky ramsky damsky
crocklefether squiggs.
        Flinkywisty pomm,
         Slushypipp

EDWARD LEAR

131

June 9

Pippen Hill

As I was going up Pippen Hill,
    Pippen Hill was dirty,
There I met a pretty miss
    And she dropped me a curtsey.

Little miss, pretty miss,
    Blessings light upon you!
If I had half-a-crown a day
    I'd spend it all upon you.

ANON

June 10

He Wishes for the Cloths of Heaven

Had I the heavens' embroidered cloths,
Enwrought with golden and silver light,
The blue and the dim and the dark cloths
Of night and light and the half-light,
I would spread the cloths under your feet:
But I, being poor, have only my dreams;
I have spread my dreams under your feet;
Tread softly because you tread on my dreams.

W. B. YEATS

June 11

The Tight Little Island

Daddy Neptune one day to Freedom did say:
If ever I live upon dry land
The spot I would hit on would be little Britain,
Says Freedom, why that's my own island.
    O what a snug little island!
    A right little tight little island!
    Search the globe round,
    None can be found
So happy as this little island.

THOMAS DIBDIN

June 12

From Young and Old

When all the world is young, lad,
    And all the trees are green;
And every goose a swan, lad,
    And every lass a queen;
Then hey for boot and horse, lad,
    And round the world away;
Young blood must have its course, lad,
    And every dog his day.

CHARLES KINGSLEY

June 13

Baby and I

Baby and I
Were baked in a pie,
The gravy was wonderful hot.
We had nothing to pay
To the baker that day
And so we crept out of the pot.

ANON

June 14

The Village Burglar

Under the spreading gooseberry bush
    The village burglar lies;
The burglar is a hairy man
    With whiskers round his eyes.

He goes to church on Sundays;
    He hears the Parson shout;
He puts a penny in the plate
    And takes a shilling out.

ANON

June 15

Daddy Fell Into the Pond

Everyone grumbled. The sky was grey.
We had nothing to do and nothing to say.
We were nearing the end of a dismal day.
And there seemed to be nothing beyond,
   Then
      Daddy fell into the pond!

And everyone's face grew merry and bright,
And Timothy danced for sheer delight.
'Give me the camera, quick, oh quick!
He's crawling out of the duckweed.' Click!

Then the gardener suddenly slapped his knee,
And doubled up, shaking silently,
And the ducks all quacked as if they were daft,
And it sounded as if the old drake laughed.
O, there wasn't a thing that didn't respond
   When
      Daddy fell into the pond!

ALFRED NOYES

June 16

The Cow

The friendly cow, all red and white,
    I love with all my heart:
She gives me cream with all her might,
    To eat with apple tart.

She wanders lowing here and there,
    And yet she cannot stray,
All in the pleasant open air,
    The pleasant light of day;

And blown by all the winds that pass
    And wet with all the showers,
She walks among the meadow grass
    And eats the meadow flowers.

ROBERT LOUIS STEVENSON

June 17

Warning

Mother, may I go out to swim?
    Yes, my darling daughter.
Hang your clothes on a hickory limb
    And don't go near the water.

ANON

June 18

The Garden Seat

Its former green is blue and thin,
And its once firm legs sink in and in;
Soon it will break down unaware,
Soon it will break down unaware.

At night when reddest flowers are black
Those who once sat thereon come back;
Quite a row of them sitting there,
Quite a row of them sitting there.

With them the seat does not break down,
Nor winter freeze them, nor floods drown,
For they are as light as upper air,
They are as light as upper air!

THOMAS HARDY

June 19

If All the Seas Were One Sea

If all the seas were one sea,
What a great sea that would be!
If all the trees were one tree,
What a great tree that would be!
And if all the axes were one axe,
What a great big axe that would be!
And if all the men were one man,
What a great man that would be!
And if the great man took the great axe
And cut down the great tree,
And let it fall into the great sea,
What a splish-splash that would be!

ANON

June 20

At the Seaside

When I was down beside the sea
A wooden spade they gave to me
   To dig the sandy shore.
My holes were empty like a cup,
In every hole the sea came up,
   Till it could come no more.

ROBERT LOUIS STEVENSON

June 21

Lavender's Blue

Lavender's blue, dilly dilly: lavender's green;
When I am King, dilly dilly, you shall be Queen.
Who told you so, dilly dilly, who told you so?
I told myself, dilly dilly, I told me so.

Call up your men, dilly dilly, set them to work;
Some to the plough, dilly dilly, some to the cart.
Some to make hay, dilly dilly, some to thresh corn,
While you and I, dilly dilly, keep ourselves warm.

If I should die, dilly dilly, as well may hap,
Bury me deep, dilly dilly, under the tap.
Under the tap, dilly dilly, I'll tell you why,
That I may drink, dilly dilly, when I am dry.

ANON

June 22

How the Sun Rose

I'll tell you how the Sun rose –
A Ribbon at a time –
The Steeples swam in Amethyst –
The news, like Squirrels, ran –
The Hills untied their Bonnets –
The Bobolinks – begun –
Then I said softly to myself –
'That must have been the Sun!'
But how he set – I know not –
There seemed a purple stile
That little Yellow boys and girls
Were climbing all the while –
Till when they reached the other side,
A Dominie in Gray –
Put gently up the evening Bars –
And led the flock away –

EMILY DICKINSON

June 23

How the Sun Set

Blazing in Gold and quenching in Purple
Leaping like Leopards to the Sky
Then at the feet of the old Horizon
Laying her spotted Face to die
Stooping as low as the Otter's Window
Touching the Roof and tinting the Barn
Kissing her Bonnet to the Meadow
And the Juggler of Day is gone

EMILY DICKINSON

June 24

Spanish Ladies

Farewell and adieu to you, Fair Spanish Ladies,
   Farewell and adieu to you, Ladies of Spain,
For we've received orders to sail for old England,
   But we hope in a short time to see you again.
     We'll rant and we'll roar, all o'er the wild ocean,
     We'll rant and we'll roar, all o'er the wild seas,
Until we strike soundings in the Channel of Old England,
   From Ushant to Scilly is thirty-five leagues.

ANON

June 25

To a Black Greyhound

Shining black in the shining light,
Inky black in the golden sun,
Graceful as the swallow's flight,
Light as a swallow, winged one,
Swift as driven hurricane,
Double-sinewed stretch and spring –
Muffled thud of flying feet –
See the black dog galloping,
Hear his wild foot-beat.

See him lie when the day is dead,
Black curves curled on the boarded floor.
Sleepy eyes, my sleepy-head –
Eyes that were aflame before.
Gentle now, they burn no more;
Gentle now and softly warm,
With the fire that made them bright
Hidden – as when after storm
Softly falls the night.

JULIAN GRENFELL

June 26

The Monkey's Wedding

The monkey married the baboon's sister,
Gave her a ring and then he kissed her,
He kissed so hard he raised a blister,
    She set up a yell.
The bridesmaid stuck on sticking-plaster,
It stuck so hard it couldn't stick faster,
That was a terrible disaster,
    But it soon got well.

What do you think they had for supper?
Chestnuts raw and boiled in butter,
Apples sliced and onions toasted,
    Peanuts not a few.
What do you think they had for a fiddle?
An old banjo with a hole in the middle,
A tambourine and a worn-out griddle,
    Hurdy-gurdy too.

ANON

June 27

Desperate Dan

Desperate Dan
The dirty old man
Washed his face
In a frying-pan.
Combed his hair
With the leg of a chair,
Desperate Dan,
The dirty old man.

ANON

June 28

Hoodoo

You remind me of a man . . .
　　What man?
A man of power . . .
　　What power?
The power of Hoodoo . . .
　　Who do?
You do . . .
　　I do what?
You remind me of a man . . .
　　What man?
A man of power . . .

ANON

June 29

The Fairy Knight (from Culprit Fay)

He put his acorn-helmet on;
It was plum'd of the silk of the thistle-down;
The corselet plate, that guarded his breast,
Was once the wild bee's golden vest;
His cloak, of a thousand mingled dyes,
Was form'd of the wings of butterflies;
His shield was the shell of a lady-bug queen,
Studs of gold on a ground of green;
And the quivering lance which he brandish'd bright,
Was the sting of a wasp he had slain in fight.

Swift he bestrode his fiery steed;
    He bared his blade of the bent grass blue;
He drove his spurs of the cockle-seed,
    And away, like a glance of thought, he flew,
To skim the heavens, and follow far
The fiery tail of the rocket star.

JOSEPH RODMAN DRAKE

June 30

from Mary's Lamb

Mary had a little lamb,
    Its fleece was white as snow,
And everywhere that Mary went
    The lamb was sure to go.
He followed her to school one day –
    That was against the rule,
It made the children laugh and play
    To see a lamb at school.

'What makes the lamb love Mary so?'
    The little children cry;
'Oh, Mary loves the lamb, you know,'
    The teacher did reply.
'And you each gentle animal
    In confidence may bind,
And make it follow at your call,
    If you are always kind.'

SARAH JOSEPHA HALE

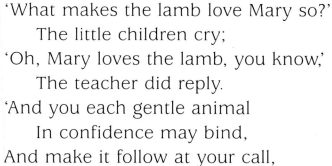

July 1
Slowly

Slowly the tide creeps up the sand,
Slowly the shadows cross the land.
Slowly the cart-horse pulls his mile,
Slowly the old man mounts the stile.

Slowly the hands move round the clock,
Slowly the dew dries on the dock.
Slow is the snail – but slowest of all
The green moss spreads on the old brick wall.

JAMES REEVES

July 2
Policeman, Policeman

Policeman, policeman, don't take me!
Take that man behind that tree!
I stole brass, he stole gold.
Policeman, policeman, don't take hold!

ANON

July 3

The Hedgehog

The Hedgehog hides beneath the rotten hedge
And makes a great round nest of grass and sedge,
Or in a bush or in a hollow tree;
And many often stoop and say they see
Him roll and fill his prickles full of crabs
And creep away; and where the magpie dabs
His wing at muddy dyke, in aged root
He makes a nest and fills it full of fruit,
On the hedge-bottom hunts for crabs and sloes
And whistles like a cricket as he goes.

JOHN CLARE

The crabs in this poem are crab-apples.

July 4

Tall Nettles

Tall nettles cover up, as they have done
These many springs, the rusty harrow, the plough
Long worn out, and the roller made of stone:
Only the elm butt tops the nettles now.

This corner of the farmyard I like most:
As well as any bloom upon a flower
I like the dust on the nettles, never lost
Except to prove the sweetness of a shower.

EDWARD THOMAS

July 5

from Ballad

The auld wife sat at her ivied door,
    (Butter and eggs and a pound of cheese)
A thing she had frequently done before;
    And her spectacles lay on her apron'd knees.

The piper he piped on the hill-top high,
    (Butter and eggs and a pound of cheese)
Till the cow said 'I die,' and the goose ask'd 'Why?'
    And the dog said nothing, but search'd for fleas.

The farmer he strode through the square farmyard;
    (Butter and eggs and a pound of cheese)
His last brew of ale was a trifle hard –
    The connexion of which with the plot one sees.

The farmer's daughter hath ripe red lips;
    (Butter and eggs and a pound of cheese)
If you try to approach her, away she skips
    Over tables and chairs with apparent ease.

The farmer's daughter hath soft brown hair
    (Butter and eggs and a pound of cheese)
And I met with a ballad, I can't say where,
    Which wholly consisted of lines like these.

CHARLES STUART CALVERLEY

July 6

The Flower-Fed Buffaloes

The flower-fed buffaloes of the spring
In the days of long ago,
Ranged where the locomotives sing
And the prairie flowers lie low:–
The tossing, blooming, perfumed grass
Is swept away by the wheat,
Wheels and wheels and wheels spin by
In the spring that still is sweet.
But the flower-fed buffaloes of the spring
Left us, long ago.
They gore no more, they bellow no more,
They trundle around the hills no more:–
With the Blackfeet, lying low,
With the Pawnees, lying low,
Lying low.

VACHEL LINDSAY

July 7

Snooks and Brooks

As Tommy Snooks and Bessy Brooks
Were walking out one Sunday,
Says Tommy Snooks to Bessy Brooks,
"Tomorrow will be Monday."

ANON

July 8

The Village Shop

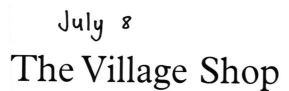

My shop is well-stocked, neat, convenient and handy;
Figs, almonds and raisins and sweet sugar candy;
Dates, currants and bull's eyes and treacle and spice,
Fine teas, barley sugar and mince pies and rice.

I've long Spanish liquorice when you've a cold
And coffee and chocolate by me are sold.
If children are good, like good children I treat them
And all my good things, O! how sweetly they eat them.

ANON

July 9

The Great Panjandrum

So she went into the garden
to cut a cabbage leaf,
to make an apple pie;
and at the same time
a great she-bear, coming down the street,
pops its head into the shop.
What! no soap?
So he died,
and she very imprudently married the Barber.
And there were present
the Picninnies,
and the Joblilies,
and the Garyulies,
and The Great Panjandrum himself,
with the little round button at top;
and they all fell to playing the game
of catch-as-catch-can,
till the gunpowder ran out at the heels of their boots.

SAMUEL FOOTE

July 10

What a Day It's Been!

Dear children, what a day it's been!
The kind of day when days
Are not what they are meant to be
In several kind of ways.

My eyes are dim for I have sobbed
Twelve tears of Platform Brine,
There'll *never* be another Niece
As innocent as mine!

Mine was the One! Mine was the Two;
Mine was the Three and Four,
And I have heard her parents say
She rose to Seven or more!

So be it. She is gone, and I
Am left at Waterloo;
Half magical, half tragical,
And, half-an-hour . . . or two.

MERVYN PEAKE

July 11

To a Ladybird

Ladybird, Ladybird,
Fly away home.
Your house is on fire
And your children are gone.
All except one –
Her name is Ann,
And she has crept under
The frying pan.

ANON

July 12

Sir Christopher Wren
Said, 'I am going to dine with some men.
If anybody calls
Say I am designing St Paul's.'

Edward the Confessor
Slept under the dresser.
When that began to pall,
He slept in the hall.

EDMUND CLERIHEW BENTLEY

July 13

Warning to Parents

Three children sliding on the ice,
   Upon a summer's day,
It so fell out they all fell in,
   The rest they ran away.

Now had these children been at home,
   Or sliding on dry ground,
Ten thousand pounds to one penny
   They had not all been drowned.

You parents all that children have,
   And you that have but none,
If you would keep them safe abroad,
   Pray keep them safe at home.

ANON

July 14

Young Henry and Mary

Henry was a young king,
    Mary was his queen;
He gave her a snowdrop
    On a stalk of green.

Then for all his kindness
    And for all his care
She gave him a new-laid egg
    In the garden there.

"Love can you sing?" – "I cannot sing."
"Or tell a tale?" – "Not one I know."
"Then let us play at queen and king
As down the garden walks we go."

ROBERT GRAVES

July 15

Unseasonable Carol

We four lads from Liverpool are:
Paul in a taxi, John in a car,
George on a scooter, tootin' his hooter,
Following Ringo Starr!

ANON

158

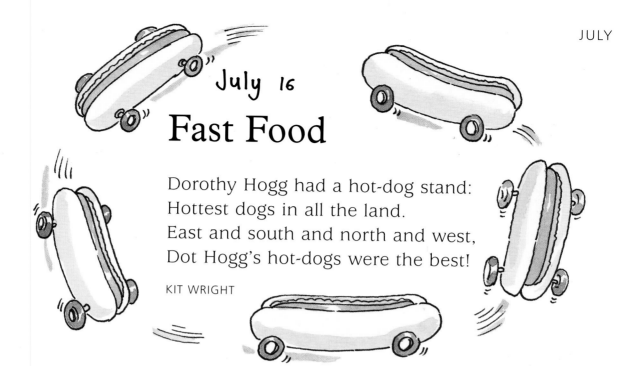

July 16

Fast Food

Dorothy Hogg had a hot-dog stand:
Hottest dogs in all the land.
East and south and north and west,
Dot Hogg's hot-dogs were the best!

KIT WRIGHT

July 17

Strawberry Pat

Sure don't they call me Strawberry Pat,
That's what I sell, to give folks pleasure.
I packs 'em neat and you may say that,
For a pint of them fills a gallon measure.
And then, to be sure, I let pass by
The world and all its curious bobberies.
Ah! see that lover there so sly.
What am I saying? Arrah, strawberries!
        Fine strawberries,
        And they're all so round,
        So fine, so sound,
They're all my scarlet strawberries.

CHARLES DIBDIN

July 18

The Greenwood

Alone in the greenwood must I roam,
    Hollin, green hollin,
A shade of green leaves is my home,
    Birk and green hollin.

Where nought is seen but boundless green,
    Hollin, green hollin,
And spots of far blue sky between,
    Birk and green hollin.

A weary head a pillow finds,
    Hollin, green hollin,
Where leaves fall green in summer winds,
    Birk and green hollin.

Enough for me, enough for me,
    Hollin, green hollin,
To live at large with liberty,
    Birk and green hollin.

ANON

July 19

Moonlight, Summer Moonlight

'Tis moonlight, summer moonlight,
All soft and still and fair;
The silent time of midnight
Shines sweetly everywhere,

But most where trees are sending
Their breezy boughs on high,
Or stooping low are lending
A shelter from the sky.

EMILY BRONTE

July 20

In the Dumps

We're all in the dumps,
For diamonds are trumps;
The kittens are gone to St Paul's!
The babies are bit,
The Moon's in a fit,
And the houses are built without walls.

ANON

July 21

A Poison Tree

I was angry with my friend:
I told my wrath, my wrath did end.
I was angry with my foe:
I told it not, my wrath did grow.

And I watered it in fears,
Night & morning with my tears;
And I sunned it with smiles,
And with soft deceitful wiles.

And it grew both day and night,
Till it bore an apple bright.
And my foe beheld it shine,
And he knew that it was mine,

And into my garden stole
When the night had veiled the pole;
In the morning glad I see
My foe outstretched beneath the tree.

WILLIAM BLAKE

July 22
Jack, Jack

Jack, Jack, the bread's burning black,
    It's burning all to a cinder.
If you don't come in and fetch it out,
    We'll throw it through the winder.

ANON

July 23
from The Cloud

I bring fresh showers for the thirsting flowers,
    From the seas and the streams;
I bear light shade for the leaves when laid
    In their noonday dreams.
From my wings are shaken the dews that waken
    The sweet buds every one,
When rocked to rest on their mother's breast,
    As she dances about the sun.
I wield the flail of the lashing hail,
    And whiten the green plains under,
And then again I dissolve it in rain,
    And laugh as I pass in thunder.

PERCY BYSSHE SHELLEY

July 24

Lost, Stolen or Strayed Notice

A little man walking about barefooted with his grandfather's boots on, carrying on his back an empty sack full of cheese. Anyone finding the same, will they please return to Mr Green, door painted red, and they will be handsomely rewarded with a yard of wood to make themselves a flannel shirt.

ANON AGAIN

July 25

The summer nights are short
   Where northern days are long:
For hours and hours lark after lark
   Trills out his song.

The summer days are short
   Where southern nights are long:
Yet short the night when nightingales
   Trill out their song.

CHRISTINA ROSSETTI

July 26

The Penny Fiddle

Yesterday I bought a penny fiddle
    And put it to my chin to play,
But I found that the strings were painted,
    So I threw my fiddle away.

A gipsy girl found my penny fiddle
    As it lay abandoned there;
When she asked me if she might keep it,
    I told her I did not care.

Then she drew such music from the fiddle
    With help of a farthing bow,
That I offered five shillings for the secret.
    But, alas, she would not let it go.

ROBERT GRAVES

July 27

The Yak

As a friend to the children commend me the Yak.
    You will find it exactly the thing:
It will carry and fetch, you can ride on its back,
    Or lead it about with a string.

The Tartar who dwells on the plains of Tibet
    (A desolate region of snow)
Has for centuries made it a nursery pet,
    And surely the Tartar should know!

Then tell your papa where the Yak can be got,
    And if he is awfully rich,
He will buy you the creature – or else he will *not*.
    (I cannot be positive which.)

HILAIRE BELLOC

July 28

Appley Dapply

Appley Dapply, a little brown mouse,
Goes to the cupboard in Somebody's house;
In Somebody's cupboard, there's everything nice –
Cake, jam and candles – delightful to mice!
Appley Dapply has little sharp eyes,
And Appley Dapply is *so* fond of pies!

BEATRIX POTTER

July 29

My Aunt She Died

My aunt she died a month ago,
    And left me all her riches,
A feather-bed and a wooden leg,
    And a pair of calico breeches.
A coffee-pot without a spout,
    A mug without a handle,
A baccy box without a lid,
    And half a farthing candle.

ANON

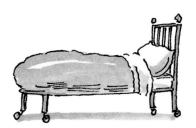

July 30

Sly Reynard the Fox

Sly Reynard sneaked out from a farmer's hen-roost,
Where a young one he'd just been a-picking;
Half strangled he looked, for he could not get loose
A bone, from his throat, of a chicken!

He twisted his jaw, and his eyes rolled about,
Like a cat in a quinsey he croaked too:
"Will no good-natured bird," he cried, "Take the bone out?"
('Twas a flock of poor geese that he spoke to).

"I'll befriend you forever," cries Reynard the Fox.
"From the weasel, cat, badger and ferret;
He that pulls out the bone that distorts my poor chops
Is a goose I'll reward for his merit!"

A gander advanced, once the pride of the flocks,
No friend of his fate could remind him,
He thrust his poor beak down the throat of the fox,
But he left his poor head there behind him!

ANON

July 31

The Key of the Kingdom

This is the key of the Kingdom:
In that Kingdom is a city;
In that city is a town;
In that town is a street;
In that street there winds a lane;
In that lane there is a yard;
In that yard there is a house;
In that house there waits a room;
In that room an empty bed;
And on that bed a basket –
A basket of sweet flowers,
    Of flowers, of flowers,
     A basket of sweet flowers.

Flowers in a basket;
Basket on the bed;
Bed in the room;
Room in the house;
House in the yard;
Yard in the winding lane;
Lane in the street;
Street in the town;
Town in the city;
City in the Kingdom –
This is the key of the Kingdom.
    Of the Kingdom this is the key.

ANON

August 1

Counting-Out

As I was walking down the lake
I met a little rattlesnake,
I gave him so much jelly-cake
It made his little belly ache –
One, two, three,
Out goes she!

ANON

August 2

Singing Game

In and out the dusty bluebells,
In and out the dusty bluebells,
In and out the dusty bluebells,
    I am the master.

Tippety, tappety, on your shoulder,
Tippety, tappety, on your shoulder,
Tippety, tappety, on your shoulder,
    I am the master.

ANON

August 3

The Sniffle

In spite of her sniffle
Isabel's chiffle.
Some girls with a sniffle
Would be weepy and tiffle;
They would look awful,
Like rained-on waffle,
But Isabel's chiffle
In spite of her sniffle.
Her nose is more red
With a cold in her head,
But then, to be sure,
Her eyes are bluer.
Some girls with a snuffle,
Their tempers are uffle.
But when Isabel's snivelly
She's snivelly civilly,
And when she's snuffly
She's perfectly luffly.

OGDEN NASH

August 4

from A Child's Dream

I had a little dog, and my dog was very small;
He licked me in the face, and he answered to my call;
Of all the treasures that were mine, I loved him most of all.

His nose was fresh as morning dew and blacker than the night;
I thought that it could even snuff the shadows and the light;
And his tail he held bravely, like a banner in a fight.

His body covered thick with hair was very good to smell;
His little stomach underneath was pink as any shell;
And I loved him and honoured him, more than words can tell.

FRANCES CORNFORD

August 5

from The Princess

The splendour falls on castle walls
     And snowy summits old in story;
The long light shakes across the lakes,
     And the wild cataract leaps in glory.
Blow, bugle, blow, set the wild echoes flying,
Blow, bugle; answer, echoes, dying, dying, dying.

O, hark, O, hear! how thin and clear,
     And thinner, clearer, farther going!
O, sweet and far from cliff and scar
     The horns of Elfland faintly blowing!
Blow, let us hear the purple glens replying,
Blow, bugle; answer, echoes, dying, dying, dying.

O love, they die in yon rich sky,
     They faint on hill or field or river;
Our echoes roll from soul to soul,
     And grow for ever and for ever.
Blow, bugle, blow, set the wild echoes flying,
And answer, echoes, answer, dying, dying, dying.

ALFRED TENNYSON

August 6

The Eagle

He clasps the crag with crooked hands;
Close to the sun in lonely lands,
Ringed with the azure world, he stands.

The wrinkled sea beneath him crawls;
He watches from his mountain walls,
And like a thunderbolt he falls.

ALFRED TENNYSON

August 7

The Octopus

Tell me, O Octopus, I begs,
Is those things arms, or is they legs?
I marvel at thee, Octopus;
If I were thou, I'd call me us.

OGDEN NASH

August 8

'Tis Midnight

'Tis midnight, and the setting sun
  Is slowly rising in the west;
The rapid rivers slowly run,
  The frog is on his downy nest.
The pensive goat and sportive cow,
Hilarious, leap from bough to bough.

ANON

August 9

from To Thomas Moore

Here's a sigh to those who love me,
  And a smile to those who hate;
And, whatever sky's above me,
  Here's a heart for every fate.

GEORGE GORDON BYRON

August 10

Swimming Pool

Floating, floating weightless
In the nothingness of pool,
I am all wet thoughts.

Water-soaked, whirling hair
Melts into my skin.
I am bathed in blue.

Nothing beneath to feel.
Nothing but sky overhead.
I live outside myself.

MYRA COHN LIVINGSTON

August 11

The Bandog

Has anybody seen my Mopser?–
   A comely dog is he,
With hair the colour of a Charles the Fifth,
   And teeth like ships at sea,
His tail it curls straight upwards,
   His ears stand two abreast,
And he answers to the simple name of Mopser,
   When civilly addressed.

WALTER DE LA MARE

August 12

Go Get the Axe

Peepin' through the knot-hole of grandpa's wooden leg,
Who'll wind the clock when I am gone?
Go get the axe – there's a flea in Lizzie's ear,
For a boy's best friend is his mother.

Peepin' through the knot-hole of grandpa's wooden leg,
Why do they build the shore so near the ocean?
Who cut the sleeves out of dear old daddy's vest,
And dug up Fido's bones to build a sewer?

A horsey stood around with his feet upon the ground,
Oh who will wind the clock when I am gone?
The cellar is behind the door, Mary's room is behind the axe,
But a boy's best friend is his mother.

ANON

August 13

New Sights

I like to see a thing I know
Has not been seen before,
That's why I cut my apple through
To look into the core.

It's nice to think, though many an eye
Has seen the ruddy skin,
Mine is the very first to spy
The five brown pips within.

ANON

August 14

from Lochinvar

O, young Lochinvar is come out of the west,
Through all the wide Border his steed was the best;
And save his good broadsword he weapons had none,
He rode all unarm'd, and he rode all alone.
So faithful in love, and so dauntless in war,
There never was a knight like the young Lochinvar.

WALTER SCOTT

August 15

The Pedlar's Caravan

I wish I lived in a caravan,
With a horse to drive, like the pedlar-man!
Where he comes from nobody knows,
Or where he goes to, but on he goes!

His caravan has windows two,
And a chimney of tin, that the smoke comes through;
He has a wife, with a baby brown,
And they go riding from town to town.

Chairs to mend, and delf to sell!
He clashes the basins like a bell;
Tea-trays, baskets ranged in order,
Plates with the alphabet round the border!

The roads are brown, and the sea is green,
But his house is just like a bathing-machine;
The world is round, and he can ride,
Rumble and splash, to the other side!

With the pedlar-man I should like to roam,
And write a book when I came home;
All the people would read my book,
Just like the Travels of Captain Cook.

WILLIAM BRIGHTY RANDS

August 16

Marigolds

I bought a bottle of Nettle Shampoo
    this morning
When I got home I wondered whether
    I shouldn't shampoo
        the marigolds
                as well.

ADRIAN HENRI

August 17

Thistle Make You Whistle

Theophilus Thistledown, the successful thistle sifter,
In sifting a sieve of unsifted thistles,
Thrust three thousand thistles
Through the thick of his thumb.
If then, Theophilus Thistledown, the successful thistle sifter,
In sifting a sieve full of unsifted thistles,
Thrust three thousand thistles
Through the thick of his thumb,
See that thou, in sifting a sieve of unsifted thistles,
Do not get the unsifted thistles stuck in thy tongue.

ANON

August 18

Windflowers

When I was little and good
I walked in the dappled wood
Where light white windflowers grew,
And hyacinths heavy and blue.

The windflowers fluttered light,
Like butterflies white and bright;
The bluebells tremulous stood
Deep in the heart of the wood.

I gathered the white and the blue,
The wild wet woodland through,
With hands too silly and small
To clasp and carry them all.

Some dropped from my hands and died
By the home-road's grassy side;
And those that my fond hands pressed
Died even before the rest.

E. NESBIT

August 19

The Fairies Sing Their Queen Titania to Sleep

You spotted snakes with double tongues,
　　Thorny hedge-hogs, be not seen;
Newts and blind-worms, do no wrong;
　　Come not near our fairy queen.

Weaving spiders, come not here;
　　Hence, you long-legg'd spinners, hence
Beetles black, approach not near,
　　Worm, nor snail, do no offence.

　　Philomel, with melody
　　Sing in our sweet lullaby;
Lulla, lulla lullaby; lulla, lulla, lullaby;
　　Never harm, Nor spell nor charm,
　　Come our lovely lady nigh;
　　So, good night, with lullaby.

WILLIAM SHAKESPEARE, FROM *A MIDSUMMER NIGHT'S DREAM*

August 20

The Watermelon Man

Watermelon! Watermelon! Red to the rind,
If you don't believe me jest pull up your blind!
    I sell to the rich, I sell to the poor,
    I sell to the lady standin' in that door.
      Watermelon, Lady!
Come and git your nice red watermelon, Lady!
    Come on, Lady, come and get 'em.
    Gotta make the picnic by two o'clock,
    No flat tires today. Come on, Lady!
I got water with the melon, red to the rind!
If you don't believe it jest pull down your blind.
    Eat the watermelon and preee-serve the rind!

ANON

August 21

Hurt no living thing,
Ladybird nor butterfly,
Nor moth with dusty wing,
Nor cricket chirping cheerily,
Nor grasshopper, so light of leap,
Nor dancing gnat,
Nor beetle fat,
Nor harmless worms that creep.

CHRISTINA ROSSETTI

August 22

Snodding

When I broke a window
And my father said,
"Are you sure you didn't do it?"
I just snodded my head.
"Are you with us or against us?"
The school bully asked.
I snodded my head
Until the danger passed.
When I tell a lie
I turn bright red,
But I feel much safer
If I only snod my head.

BRIAN PATTEN

August 23

A Birthday

My heart is like a singing bird
    Whose nest is in a water'd shoot;
My heart is like an apple tree
    Whose boughs are bent with thick-set fruit;
My heart is like a rainbow shell
    That paddles in a halcyon sea;
My heart is gladder than all these
    Because my love is come to me.

Raise me a dais of silk and down;
    Hang it with vair and purple dyes;
Carve it in doves and pomegranates,
    And peacocks with a hundred eyes;
Work it in gold and silver grapes,
    In leaves and silver fleurs-de-lys;
Because the birthday of my life
    Is come, my love is come to me.

CHRISTINA ROSSETTI

August 24

from Merlin and the Gleam

O young Mariner,
You from the haven
Under the sea-cliff,
You that are watching
The grey Magician
With eyes of wonder,
I am Merlin,
And I am dying,
I am Merlin
Who follow The Gleam.

Mighty the Wizard
Who found me at sunrise
Sleeping, and woke me
And learned me Magic!
Great the Master,
And sweet the Magic,
When over the valley,
In early summers,
Over the mountain,
On human faces,
And all around me,
Moving to melody,
Floated The Gleam.

ALFRED TENNYSON

August 25

O Sailor, come ashore,
　　What have you brought for me?
Red coral, white coral,
　　Coral from the sea.

I did not dig it from the ground,
　　Nor pluck it from a tree;
Feeble insects made it
　　In the stormy sea.

CHRISTINA ROSSETTI

August 26

Don't Dilly-Dally on the Way

My old man said, 'Follow the van,
Don't dilly-dally on the way!'
Off went the cart with the home packed in it,
I walked behind with my old cock linnet.
But I dillied and dallied, dallied and dillied,
Lost the van and don't know where to roam.
And you can't trust the 'Specials' like the old time
　'Coppers'
When you can't find your way home.

CHARLES COLLINS

August 27

Old Adam

I'm sorry for old Adam,
Just as sorry as can be,
For he never had no mammy
For to hold him on her knee.

And he never had no childhood,
Playin' round the cabin door,
And he never had no daddy
For to tell him what he's for.

And I've always had the feelin'
He'd a let that apple be,
If he'd only had a mammy
For to hold him on her knee.

ANON

August 28

I Saw a Ship A-Sailing

I saw a ship a-sailing,
    A-sailing on the sea,
And oh but it was laden
    With pretty things for me.

There were comfits in the cabin,
    And sweetmeats in the hold;
The sails were made of silk
    And the masts were all of gold.

The four-and-twenty sailors,
    That stood between the decks,
Were four-and-twenty white mice
    With chains around their necks.

The captain was a duck
    With a jacket on his back,
And when the ship began to move
    The captain said: Quack! Quack!

ANON

August 29

Old Joe Clarke

Old Joe Clarke, he had a house
Was fifteen stories high,
And every darn room in that house
Was full of chicken pie.

I went down to Old Joe Clarke's
And found him eating supper;
I stubbed my toe on the table leg
And stuck my nose in the butter.

I went down to Old Joe Clarke's,
Old Joe wasn't in.
I sat right down on the red-hot stove
And got right up again.

ANON

August 30

There was a young lady of Ryde
Who ate some green apples and died.
    Those apples fermented
    Inside the lamented,
Making cider inside her inside.

ANON

August 31

'Tis the The Voice of the Lobster

'Tis the voice of the Lobster; I heard him declare,
'You have baked me too brown, I must sugar my hair.'
As a duck with its eyelids, so he with his nose
Trims his belt and his buttons, and turns out his toes.

When the sands are all dry, he is gay as a lark,
And will talk in contemptuous tones of the Shark:
But, when the tide rises and sharks are around,
His voice has a timid and tremulous sound.

I passed by his garden, and marked, with one eye,
How the Owl and the Panther were sharing a pie:
The Panther took pie-crust, and gravy, and meat,
While the Owl had the dish as its share of the treat.

When the pie was all finished, the Owl, as a boon,
Was kindly permitted to pocket the spoon:
While the Panther received knife and fork with a growl,
And concluded the banquet by —

LEWIS CARROLL

191

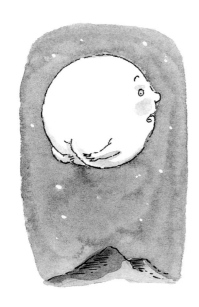

September 1

To The Moon

Oh Moon, when I look on thy beautiful face,
Careering along through the boundaries of space,
The thought has quite frequently come to my
    mind,
If ever I'll gaze on thy glorious behind.

ANON

September 2

from Wynken, Blynken, and Nod

Wynken, Blynken, and Nod one night,
    Sailed off in a wooden shoe –
Sailed on a river of crystal light,
    Into a sea of dew.
"Where are you going, and what do you wish?"
    The old moon asked the three.
"We have come to fish for the herring fish
    That live in this beautiful sea –
Nets of silver and gold have we!'
    Said Wynken,
    Blynken,
    And Nod.

EUGENE FIELD

September 3

from Rain in Summer

How beautiful is the rain!
After the dust and heat,
In the broad and fiery street,
In the narrow lane,
How beautiful is the rain!

How it clatters along the roofs,
Like the tramp of hoofs!
How it gushes and struggles out
From the throat of the overflowing spout!

Across the window pane
It pours and pours;
And swift and wide,
With a muddy tide,
Like a river down the gutter roars
The rain, the welcome rain!

HENRY WADSWORTH LONGFELLOW

September 4

A Good Poem

I like a good poem
one with lots of fighting
in it. Blood, and the
clanging of armour. Poems

against Scotland are good,
and poems that defeat
the French with crossbows.
I don't like poems that

aren't about anything.
Sonnets are wet and
a waste of time.
Also poems that don't

know how to rhyme.
If I was a poem
I'd play football and
get picked for England.

ROGER MCGOUGH

September 5

The Barkday Party

For my dog's birthday party
I dressed like a bear.
My friends came as lions
and tigers and wolves and monkeys.
At first, Runabout couldn't believe
the bear was really me. But
he became his old self again
when I fitted on his magician's top hat.
Runabout became the star, running about
jumping up on chairs and tables
barking at every question asked him.
Then, in their ordinary clothes,
my friend Brian and his dad arrived
with their boxer, Skip. And with us
knowing nothing about it, Brian's dad
mixed the dog's party meat and milk
with wine he brought. We started
singing. Runabout started to yelp.
All the other six dogs joined –
yelping
> *Happy Barkday to you*
> *Happy Barkday to you*
> *Happy Barkday Runabout*
> *Happy Barkday to you!*

JAMES BERRY

September 6

Bad Day

Nobody loves me,
Everybody hates me,
Going in the garden to eat worms.
Big fat juicy ones,
Little squiggly niggly ones,
Going in the garden to eat worms.

ANON

September 7

The Song of the Black Bryony Fairy

Bright and wild and beautiful
For the Autumn festival,
I will hang from tree to tree
Wreaths and ropes of Bryony,
To the glory and the praise
Of the sweet September days.

(There is nothing black about this Bryony, but people do say
it has a black root. This may be true, but you would need to dig
it up to find out. It used to be thought a cure for freckles).

CICELY M. BARKER

September 8

from Two Opinions

A noisy chattering Magpie once,
A talking, gabbling, hairbrained dunce,
    Came by where a sign-post stood.
He nodded his head with a modish air
And said "Good-day" for he wasn't aware
That the sign-post pointing its finger there
    Was only a block of wood.

So on he chattered with never a stop,
And on and on till you'd think he would drop –
    (The post was dumb as your hat).
So long as the magpie could say his say,
He didn't care whether it spoke all day,
For thus he observed as he walked away –
    "An intelligent creature, that!"

HOWARD PYLE

197

September 9

Stupidity Street

I saw with open eyes
Singing birds sweet
Sold in the shops
For the people to eat,
Sold in the shops of
Stupidity Street.

I saw in vision
The worm in the wheat,
And in the shops nothing
For people to eat;
Nothing for sale in
Stupidity Street.

RALPH HODGSON

September 10

Riddle

In marble halls as white as milk,
Lined with a skin as soft as silk,
Within a fountain crystal-clear,
A golden apple doth appear.
No doors there are to this stronghold,
Yet thieves break in and steal the gold.

ANON

September 11

The Vixen

Among the taller wood with ivy hung,
The old fox plays and dances round her young.
She snuffs and barks if any passes by
And swings her tail and turns prepared to fly.
The horseman hurries by, she bolts to see,
And turns agen, from danger never free.
If any stands she runs among the poles
And barks and snaps and drives them in the holes.
The shepherd sees them and the boy goes by
And gets a stick and progs the hole to try.
They get all still and lie in safety sure,
And out again when everything's secure,
And start and snap at blackbirds bouncing by
To fight and catch the great white butterfly.

JOHN CLARE

September 12

The Tragical Death of an Apple Pie

A Apple Pie.
B bit it, C cut it, D dealt it, E eat it.
F fought for it, G got it, H had it, I imagined it!
J juggled with it, K kept it, L longed for it, M mourned for it.
N nodded at it, O opened it, P peeped in it, Q quartered it.
R ran for it. S stole it. T took it. V viewed it. W wanted it.
X, Y, Z and &, they all wished for a piece in hand.

At last they every one agreed,
Upon the Apple Pie to feed;
But as there seemed to be so many,
Those who were last might not have any.
And so I watched them carefully, I did,
To see the Pie fairly divided.

ANON

September 13

The Scottish Sport

The bonniest sport in the world I must sing
All sportsmen acknowledge that fitba's the King
And wherever a boot takes a swing at a ball
It's Scotland the Brave that's the flower of them all.

    The beautiful game was by Scotland invented
    The game that has driven the world half demented
    Forget aboot Germany also Brazil
    When Scotland plays England it's always six-nil!

Ye can talk of your Cruyffs, Bobby Robsons and Peles –
Compared with oor Scots, there's nae fire in their bellies.
The soccer world trembles when our team unleash
The Sons of Bill Shankley and Kenny Dalglish.

    The beautiful game was by Scotland invented . . .

ADRIAN MITCHELL (HALF-SCOTTISH)

September 14

The Devil

From his brimstone bed at the break of day
A walking the Devil is gone
To visit his snug little farm, the earth
And see how his stock goes on.

Over the hill and over the dale,
And he went over the plain,
And backward and forward he switched his long tail
As a gentleman switches his cane.

And how then was the Devil dressed?
Oh! he was in his Sunday's best:
His jacket was red and his breeches were blue
And there was a hole where the tail came through.

SAMUEL TAYLOR COLERIDGE

September 15

from The Two Rats

He was a rat, and she was a rat,
    And down in one hole they did dwell,
And both were as black as a witch's cat,
    And they loved one another well.

He had a tail, and she had a tail,
    Both long and curling and fine;
And each said, 'Yours is the finest tail
    In the world, excepting mine.'

ANON

September 16

Money

O money is the meat in the coconut,
O money is the milk in the jug;
    When you've got lots of money
    You feel very funny,
You're happy as a bug in a rug –
        Ho Ho!
You're happy as a bug in a rug!

ANON

September 17

Sweet and Low

Sweet and low, sweet and low,
  Wind of the western sea,
Low, low, breathe and blow,
  Wind of the western sea!
Over the rolling waters go,
Come from the dying moon, and blow,
  Blow him again to me,
While my little one, while my pretty one sleeps.

Sleep and rest, sleep and rest,
  Father will come to thee soon;
Rest, rest on mother's breast,
  Father will come to thee soon;
Father will come to his babe in the nest,
Silver sails all out of the west
  Under the silver moon.
Sleep, my little one, sleep, my pretty one, sleep.

ALFRED TENNYSON

September 18

The horses of the sea
    Rear a foaming crest,
But the horses of the land
    Serve us the best.

The horses of the land
    Munch corn and clover,
While the foaming sea-horses
    Toss and turn over.

CHRISTINA ROSSETTI

September 19

Searching for the Scarlet Pimpernel

We seek him here, we seek him there,
Those Frenchies seek him everywhere.
Is he in heaven? Is he in hell?
That damned, elusive Pimpernel?

EMMUSKA ORCZY

September 20

Eutopia

There is a garden where lilies
    And roses are side by side;
And all day between them in silence
    The silken butterflies glide.

I may not enter the garden,
    Tho' I know the road thereto;
And morn by morn to the gateway
    I see the children go.

They bring back light on their faces;
    But they cannot bring back to me
What the lilies say to the roses
    Or the songs of the butterflies be.

FRANCIS TURNER PALGRAVE

September 21

The Scottish Earwig

The horny goloch is an awesome beast,
    Supple and scaly;
It has two horns, and a hantle of feet,
    And a forkie tailie.

ANON

September 22

Dawlish Fair

Over the hill and over the dale,
    And over the Bourne to Dawlish,
Where ginger-bread wives have a scanty sale,
    And ginger-bread nuts are smallish.

JOHN KEATS

September 23

Autumn Fires

In the other gardens
    And all up the vale,
From the autumn bonfires
    See the smoke trail!

Pleasant summer over
    And all the summer flowers,
The red fire blazes,
    The grey smoke towers.

Sing a song of seasons!
    Something bright in all!
Flowers in the summer,
    Fires in the fall!

ROBERT LOUIS STEVENSON

September 24

My Cats

I like to toss him up and down
A heavy cat weighs half a Crown
With a hey do diddle my cat Brown.

I like to pinch him on the sly
When nobody is passing by
With a hey do diddle my cat Fry.

I like to ruffle up his pride
And watch him skip and turn aside
With a hey do diddle my cat Hyde.

Hey Brown and Fry and Hyde my cats
That sit on tombstones for your mats.

STEVIE SMITH

September 25

My Uncle Jehosaphat

My Uncle Jehosaphat had a pig,
    A pig of high degree;
And it always wore a brown scratch wig,
    Most beautiful for to see.

My Uncle Jehosaphat loved that pig,
    And the piggy-wig loved him;
And they both jumped into the lake one day,
    To see which best could swim.

My Uncle Jehosaphat he swam up,
    And the piggy-wig he swam down;
And so they both did win the prize,
    Which the same was a velvet gown.

ANON

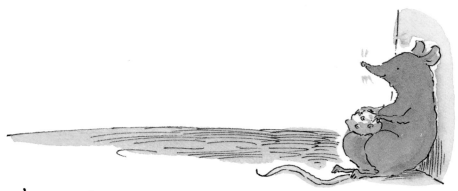

September 26

What on Earth are You Doing Here, Marvellous Mouse?

What on earth are you doing here, Marvellous Mouse,
    sitting beside the wall
with one crumb of cheese balanced on your small knees?
    Do you not think it might fall?

I am sitting here balancing cheese on my knees
    answered the Marvellous Mouse
In order to see if a new friend might be
    attracted, and come to my house.

But if I sit here all, all the night long
    awaiting my unknown friend
I know very well I'll succumb to the smell
    and eat it myself in the end.

GEORGE BARKER

September 27

Symphony in Yellow

An omnibus across the bridge
Crawls like a yellow butterfly,
And, here and there, a passer-by
Shows like a little restless midge.

Big barges full of yellow hay
Are moved against the shadowy wharf,
And, like a yellow silken scarf,
The thick fog hangs along the quay.

The yellow leaves begin to fade
And flutter from the Temple elms,
And at my feet the pale green Thames
Lies like a rod of rippled jade.

OSCAR WILDE

September 28

O Mary Don't You Weep

If I could I surely would
Stand on the rock where Moses stood.

Pharaoh's army got drownded –
O Mary don't you weep.
O Mary don't you weep, don't you mourn,
O Mary don't you weep, don't you mourn,
Pharaoh's army got drownded –
O Mary don't you weep.

The Lord told Moses what to do
To lead those Hebrew children through.
Pharaoh's army got drownded . . .

God sent Noah the rainbow sign –
No more water but the fire next time.
Pharaoh's army got drownded . . .

One of these days 'bout twelve o'clock
This old world's gonna reel and rock –
Pharaoh's army got drownded –
O Mary don't you weep . . .

ANON

213

September 29

To My Dog

This gentle beast
This golden beast
laid her long chin
along my wrist

and my wrist
is branded
with her love
and trust

and the salt of my cheek
is hers to lick
so long as I
or she shall last

ADRIAN MITCHELL

September 30

The Big Ship Sails

Oh the big ship sails on the alley alley oh,
    The alley alley oh, the alley alley oh,
The big ship sails on the alley alley oh,
    On the last day of September.

We all dip our heads in the deep blue sea,
    The deep blue sea, the deep blue sea,
We all dip our heads in the deep blue sea,
    On the last day of September.

The Captain said 'This will never never do,
    Never never do, never never do.'
The Captain said 'This will never never do,'
    On the last day of September.

The big ship sank to the bottom of the sea,
    Bottom of the sea, bottom of the sea,
The big ship sank to the bottom of the sea,
    On the last day of September.

ANON

October 1

After the Ball

After the ball was over
She lay on the sofa and sighed.
She put her false teeth in salt water
And took out her lovely glass eye.
She kicked her cork leg in the corner
And hung up her wig on the wall,
The rest of her went to bye-byes,
    After the ball.

ANON

October 2

Sun a-shine, rain a-fall

Sun a-shine an' rain a-fall,
The Devil an' him wife cyan 'gree at all,
The two o' them want one fish-head,
The Devil call him wife bonehead,
She hiss her teeth, call him cock-eye,
Greedy, worthless an' workshy,
While them busy callin' name,
The puss walk in, sey is a shame
To see a nice fish go to was'e,
Lef' with a big grin pon him face.

VALERIE BLOOM

October 3

I Was Born Almost Ten Thousand Years Ago

I was born almost ten thousand years ago,
And there's nothing in the world that I don't know;
I saw Peter, Paul and Moses
Playing ring-around-the-roses
And I'm here to lick the guy what says 'taint so.

I saw Satan when he looked the garden o'er,
Saw Adam and Eve driven from the door,
And behind the bushes peeping,
Saw the apple they were eating,
And I'll swear that I'm the guy what ate the core.

ANON

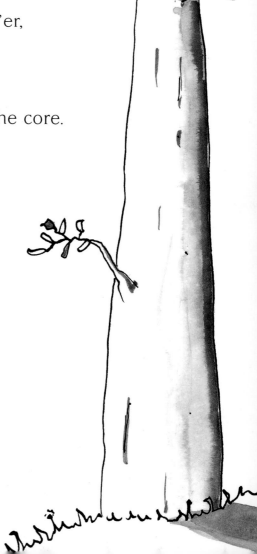

October 4

Any Old Iron?

Any old iron, any old iron,
Any any any old iron?
You look neat
Talk about a treat
You look dapper from your napper to your feet.
Dressed in style, brand new tile,
And your father's old green tie on,
But I wouldn't give you tuppence for your old watch chain –
Old iron, old iron!

CHARLES COLLINS

October 5

Try Again

I had a young man,
He was double-jointed,
When I kissed him
He was disappointed.

When he died
I had another one,
God bless his little heart,
I found a better one.

ANON

October 6

Saint Francis and the Birds

When Francis preached love to the birds
They listened, fluttered, throttled up
Into the blue like a flock of words

Released for fun from his holy lips.
Then wheeled back, whirred about his head,
Pirouetted on brothers' capes,

Danced on the wing, for sheer joy played
And sang, like images took flight.
Which was the best poem Francis made,

His argument true, his tone light.

SEAMUS HEANEY

October 7

Autumn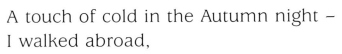

A touch of cold in the Autumn night –
I walked abroad,
And saw the ruddy moon lean over a hedge
Like a red-faced farmer.
I did not stop to speak, but nodded,
And round about were the wistful stars
With white faces like town children.

T. E. HULME

October 8

Though our barns are filled with plenty,
Wine, and oil, and golden sheaves,
Every heart hath its own burden,
Every life its Autumn leaves;
Then while sunset golde and purple
O'er the earth its glory weaves,
Let us, with the happy children
Gather up our Autumn leaves.

JOHN ANDREWS

October 9

from Endymion

A thing of beauty is a joy for ever:
Its loveliness increases, it will never
Pass into nothingness; but still will keep
A bower quiet for us, and a sleep
Full of sweet dreams, and health, and quiet breathing.
Therefore, on every morrow, are we wreathing
A flowery band to bind us to the earth,
Spite of despondence, of the inhuman dearth
Of noble natures, of the gloomy days,
Of all the unhealthy and o'er-darkened ways
Made of our searching; yes, in spite of all,
Some shape of beauty moves away the pall
From our dark spirits.

JOHN KEATS

October 10

I've Been Working on the Railroad

I've been workin' on the railroad all the livelong day,
I've been workin' on the railroad just to pass the time away.
Can't you hear the whistle blowin'? Rise up so early in the morn.
Can't you hear the captain shouting: "Dinah, blow your horn!"

Dinah won't you blow, Dinah won't you blow,
Dinah won't you blow your horn?
Dinah won't you blow, Dinah won't you blow,
Dinah won't you blow your horn?

Someone's in the kitchen with Dinah
Someone's in the kitchen I know
Someone's in the kitchen with Dinah
Strummin' on the old banjo.

A-playin' fee fi fiddle-y-o
Fee fi fiddle-y-i-o-o-o-o
Fee fi fiddle-y-i-o –
Strummin' on the old banjo.

ANON

October 11

Sneeze on a Monday

Sneeze on a Monday, you sneeze for danger,
Sneeze on a Tuesday, kiss a stranger,
Sneeze on a Wednesday, sneeze for a letter,
Sneeze on a Thursday, something better,
Sneeze on a Friday, sneeze for sorrow,
Sneeze on a Saturday, see your sweetheart
tomorrow.

ANON

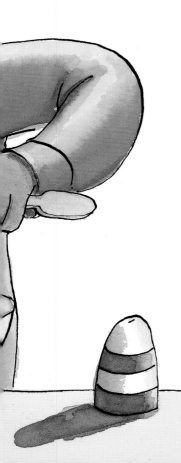

October 12

Wonky Limerick

There was an old man from Dunoon
Who always ate soup with a fork.
    For he said: "As I eat
    Neither fish, fowl, nor flesh,
I should otherwise finish too quick."

ANON

October 13

Skipping Rhyme

The wind and the wind and the wind blows high,
The rain comes scattering from the sky;
Dipsey Mitchell says she'll die
For the lad with the roving eye.

She is handsome, she is pretty,
She is the girl of the Golden City;
She has lovers, one, two, three,
Pray tell me who they'll be.

Andy Harvey says he loves her,
All the boys a fighting for her;
Let them all say what they will,
Andy Harvey has her still.

Lead her by the lily-white hand,
Lead her by the water,
Give her kisses, one, two, three,
For Mrs Mitchell's daughter.

ANON

October 14

The Loch Ness Monster's Song

Sssnnnwhuffffll?
Hnwhuffl hhnnwfl hnfl hfl?
Gdroblboblhobngbl gbl gl g g g g glbgl.
Drublhaflablhaflubhafgabhaflhafl fl fl –
gm grawwwww grf grawf awfgm graw gm.
Hovoplodok-doplodovok-plovodokot-doplodokosh?
Splgraw fok fok splgrafhatchgabrlgabrl fok splfok!
Zgra kra gka fok!
Grof grawff gahf?
Gombl mbl bl –
blm plm,
blm plm,
blm plm,
blp.

EDWIN MORGAN

October 15

The Fallow Deer at the Lonely House

One without looks in to-night
    Through the curtain-chink
From the sheet of glistening white;
One without looks in to-night
    As we sit and think
    By the fender-brink.

We do not discern those eyes
    Watching in the snow;
Lit by lamps of rosy dyes
We do not discern those eyes
    Wondering, aglow,
    Fourfooted, tiptoe.

THOMAS HARDY

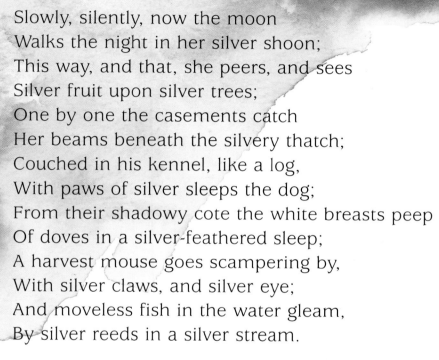

October 16

Silver

Slowly, silently, now the moon
Walks the night in her silver shoon;
This way, and that, she peers, and sees
Silver fruit upon silver trees;
One by one the casements catch
Her beams beneath the silvery thatch;
Couched in his kennel, like a log,
With paws of silver sleeps the dog;
From their shadowy cote the white breasts peep
Of doves in a silver-feathered sleep;
A harvest mouse goes scampering by,
With silver claws, and silver eye;
And moveless fish in the water gleam,
By silver reeds in a silver stream.

WALTER DE LA MARE

October 17

Hoddley, Poddley

Hoddley, poddley, puddle and frogs,
Cats are to marry the poodle dogs;
Cats in blue jackets and dogs in red hats,
What will become of the mice and rats?

ANON

October 18

Leave Her, Johnny

I thought I heard the captain say:
  Leave her, Johnny, leave her!
You may go ashore and touch your pay,
  It's time for us to leave her.

The winds were foul, the trip was long;
  Leave her, Johnny, leave her;
But before we go we'll sing a song,
  It's time for us to leave her.

The winds were foul, the work was hard –
  Leave her, Johnny, leave her;
From Liverpool Docks to Brooklyn Yard;
  It's time for us to leave her.

She'd neither steer, nor stay, nor wear;
  Leave her, Johnny, leave her;
She shipped it green and made us swear;
  It's time for us to leave her.

She'd neither wear, nor steer, nor stay;
  Leave her, Johnny, leave her;
Her running rigging carried away:
  It's time for us to leave her.

ANON

October 19

Miss Jessica and Sugar

Miss Jessica love sugar is a shame
Miss Jessica know every sweetie name
Miss Jessica no 'fraid diabetes
Miss Jessica keep sucking sweeties
Miss Jessica brush off all coconut drop
Miss Jessica gwaps down soursop
Miss Jessica no have sweet tooth tho'
she lef dem dung de dentist long time ago.

PAULINE STEWART

October 20

from The Fens

Among the tawny tasselled reed
The ducks and ducklings float and feed.
With head oft dabbing in the flood
They fish all day the weedy mud,
And tumbler-like are bobbing there,
Heels topsy-turvy in the air,
Then up and quack and down they go.
Heels over head again below.

JOHN CLARE

October 21

from The War Song of Dinas Vawr

The mountain sheep are sweeter,
But the valley sheep are fatter;
We therefore deemed it meeter
To carry off the latter.
We made an expedition;
We met a host and quelled it;
We forced a strong position,
And killed the men who held it.

On Dyfed's richest valley,
Where herds of kine were browsing,
We made a mighty sally,
To furnish our carousing.
Fierce warriors rushed to meet us;
We met them and o'erthrew them:
They struggled hard to beat us;
But we conquered them and slew them.

THOMAS LOVE PEACOCK

October 22

Witches' Charm

The owl is abroad, the bat and the toad,
　　And so is the cat-a-mountain,
The ant and the mole both sit in a hole,
　　And frog peeps out o' the fountain,
The dogs they do bay, and the timbrels play,
　　The spindle is now a-turning;
The moon it is red, and the stars are fled,
　　But all the sky is a-burning.

BEN JONSON, FROM THE MASQUE OF QUEENS

October 23

The Cat of Cats

I am the cat of cats. I am
　　The everlasting cat!
Cunning, and old, and sleek as jam,
　　The everlasting cat!
I hunt the vermin in the night –
　　The everlasting cat!
For I see best without the light –
　　The everlasting cat!

WILLIAM BRIGHTY RANDS

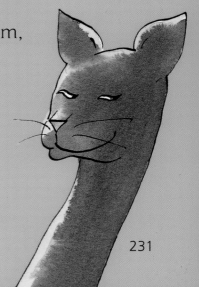

October 24

from Kubla Khan,
 A Vision in a Dream

In Xanadu did Kubla Khan
A stately pleasure dome decree:
Where Alph, the sacred river, ran
Through caverns measureless to man
  Down to a sunless sea.
So twice five miles of fertile ground
With walls and towers were girdled round:
And there were gardens bright with sinuous rills,
Where blossomed many an incense-bearing tree;
And here were forests ancient as the hills,
Enfolding sunny spots of greenery.

But oh! that deep romantic chasm which slanted
Down the green hill athwart a cedarn cover!
A savage place! as holy and enchanted
As e'er beneath a waning moon was haunted
By woman wailing for her demon lover!

SAMUEL TAYLOR COLERIDGE

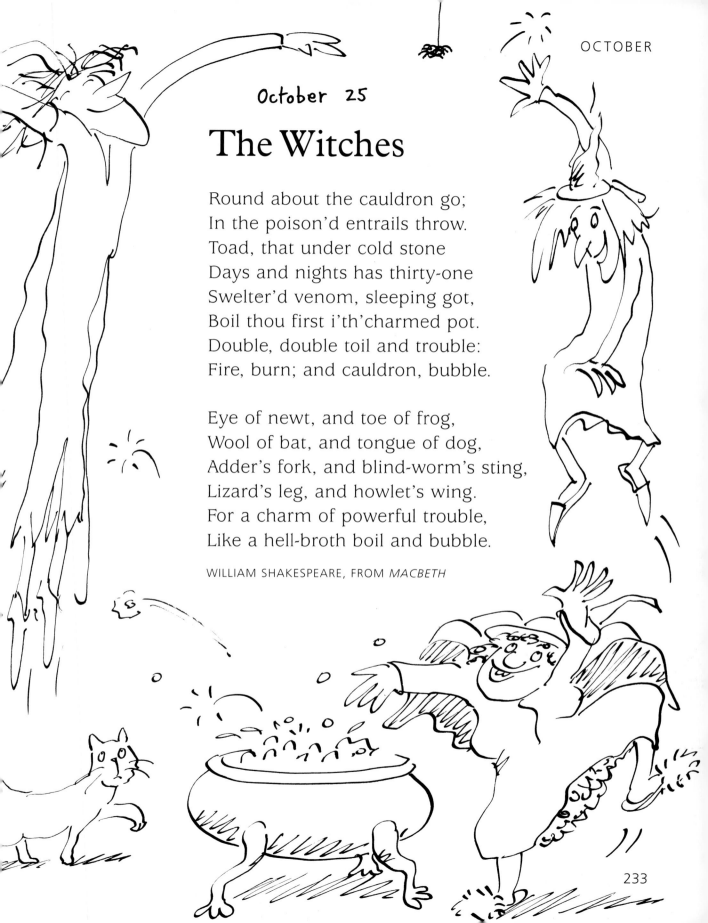

October 25

The Witches

Round about the cauldron go;
In the poison'd entrails throw.
Toad, that under cold stone
Days and nights has thirty-one
Swelter'd venom, sleeping got,
Boil thou first i'th'charmed pot.
Double, double toil and trouble:
Fire, burn; and cauldron, bubble.

Eye of newt, and toe of frog,
Wool of bat, and tongue of dog,
Adder's fork, and blind-worm's sting,
Lizard's leg, and howlet's wing.
For a charm of powerful trouble,
Like a hell-broth boil and bubble.

WILLIAM SHAKESPEARE, FROM *MACBETH*

October 26

Everyone Sang

Everyone suddenly burst out singing;
And I was filled with such delight
As prisoned birds must find in freedom
Winging wildly across the white
Orchards and dark green fields; on; on;
    and out of sight.

Everyone's voice was suddenly lifted,
And beauty came like the setting sun,
My heart was shaken with tears and horror
Drifted away . . . O but every one
Was a bird; and the song was wordless; the singing
    will never be done.

SIEGFRIED SASSOON

October 27

Counting-Out

Ibbity, bibbity, sibbity, sab,
Ibbity, bibbity, canal-boat.
    Dictionary;
    Down the ferry;
    Fun! Fun!
    American gun!
Eighteen hundred and sixty one!

ANON

October 28

Shoo fly

Shoo fly, don't bother me,
Shoo fly, don't bother me,
Shoo fly, don't bother me –
I belong to somebody.

I feel, I feel,
I feel like a morning star.
I feel, I feel,
I feel like a morning star.

Shoo fly, don't bother me . . .

ANON

October 29

Rosy Apple, Lemon or Pear

Rosy apple, lemon or pear,
Bunch of roses she shall wear;
Gold and silver by her side,
I know who will be the bride.
Take her by the lily-white hand.
    Lead her to the altar;
Give her kisses – one, two, three –
    Mother's runaway daughter.

ANON

October 30

Autumn Birds

The wild duck startles like a sudden thought,
And heron slow as if it might be caught.
The flopping crows on weary wings go by,
And grey beard jackdaws noising as they fly.
The crowds of starnels whizz and hurry by,
And darken like a cloud the evening sky.
The larks like thunder rise and suthy round,
Then drop and nestle in the stubble ground.
The wild swan hurries high and noises loud
With white neck peering to the evening cloud.
The weary rooks to distant woods are gone.
With lengths of tail the magpie winnows on
To neighbouring tree, and leaves the distant crows,
While small birds nestle in the hedge below.

JOHN CLARE

October 31 Halloween

Lazy Witch

Lazy witch,
What's wrong with you?
Get up and stir your magic brew.
Here's candlelight to chase the gloom.
Jump up and mount your flying broom
And muster up your charms and spells
And wicked grins and piercing yells.
It's Halloween! There's work to do!
Lazy witch,
What's wrong with you?

MYRA COHN LIVINGSTON

Punkie Night

It's Punkie Night tonight,
It's Punkie Night tonight,
Give us a candle, give us a light,
It's Punkie Night tonight.

ANON

237

November 1

Abalone

O some folks boast of quail on toast
Because they think it's toney,
But my old tom-cat gets good and fat
On hunks of abalone.

Some folks say that pain is real
And some say that it's phoney;
But as for me, I can't agree,
I eat an abalone.

ANON

November 2

Rooster and Chicken

Rooster and Chicken had a fight,
Chicken knocked Rooster out of sight.
Rooster told Chicken, that's all right,
I'll meet you in the stewpot Sunday night.

Once upon a time, the rooster drank wine,
The monkey played the fiddle on the streetcar line.
The streetcar broke, the monkey got choked
And they all went to heaven in a little rowboat.

ANON

November 3

from The Daisy

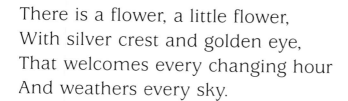

There is a flower, a little flower,
With silver crest and golden eye,
That welcomes every changing hour
And weathers every sky.

It smiles upon the lap of May,
Lights pale October on its way,
And twines December's arms.

JAMES MONTGOMERY

November 4

Rain on the Down

Night, and the down by the sea,
And the veil of rain on the down;
And she came through the mist and the rain to me
From the safe warm lights of the town.

The rain shone in her hair,
And her face gleam'd in the rain;
And only the night and the rain were there
As she came to me out of the rain.

ARTHUR SYMONS

November 5

"Please to Remember"

Here am I,
A poor old Guy:
Legs in a bonfire,
Head in the sky,

Shoeless my toes,
Wild stars behind,
Smoke in my nose,
And my eye-peeps blind;

Old hat, old straw –
In this disgrace;
While the wildfire gleams
On a mask for face.

Ay, all I am made of
Only trash is;
And soon – soon,
Will be dust and ashes.

WALTER DE LA MARE

November 6

Belagcholly Days
(with a heavy cold)

Chilly Dovebber with his boadigg blast
    Dow cubs add strips the bedow add the lawd,
Eved October's suddy days are past –
    Add Subber's gawd!

I kdow dot what it is to which I cligg
    That stirs to sogg add sorrow, yet I trust
That still I sigg, but as the liddets sigg –
    Because I bust . . .

Farewell, by cherished strolliggs od the sward,
    Greed glades and forest shades, farewell to you;
With sorrowing heart I, wretched add forlord,
    Bid you – achew!!!

ANON

November 7

Small, Smaller

I thought that I knew all there was to know
Of being small, until I saw once, black against the snow,
A shrew, trapped in my footprint, jump and fall
And jump again and fall, the hole too deep, the walls too tall.

RUSSELL HOBAN

November 8

They are slaves who will not choose
Hatred, scoffing and abuse,
Rather than in silence shrink
From the truth they needs must think;
They are slaves who dare not be
In the right with two or three.

JAMES RUSSELL LOWELL

November 9

There was an old man of Khartoum
Who kept a tame sheep in his room.
   "To remind me," he said,
   "Of someone who's dead,
But I never can recollect whom."

ANON

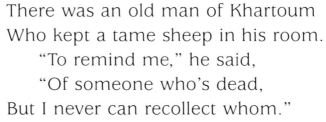

November 10

If All The World Were Paper

If all the world were paper,
And all the seas were ink,
If all the trees were bread and cheese,
What should we do for drink?

If all our vessels ran aground
Upon a rock in China,
If Spanish apes ate all the grapes,
How should we do for wine-a?

If all the world were men,
And men all lived in trenches,
And there were none but men alone,
What should they do for wenches?

If there had been no lovers,
Nor none that did great wrongs,
If fiddlers all go play football,
How should we do for songs?

ANON

November 11

from The Pobble Who Has No Toes

The Pobble who has no toes
    Had once as many as we;
When they said, 'Some day you may lose them all;' –
    He replied, – 'Fish fiddle de-dee!'
And his Aunt Jobiska made him drink,
Lavender water tinged with pink,
For she said, 'The World in general knows
There's nothing so good for a Pobble's toes!'

The Pobble who has no toes,
    Swam across the Bristol Channel;
But before he set out he wrapped his nose,
    In a piece of scarlet flannel.
For his Aunt Jobiska said, 'No harm
Can come to his toes if his nose is warm;
And it's perfectly known that a Pobble's toes
Are safe, – provided he minds his nose.'

The Pobble swam fast and well
    And when boats or ships came near him
He tinkledy-binkledy-winkled a bell
    So that all the world could hear him.
And all the Sailors and Admirals cried,
When they saw him nearing the further side, –
'He has gone to fish, for his Aunt Jobiska's
Runcible Cat with crimson whiskers!'

EDWARD LEAR

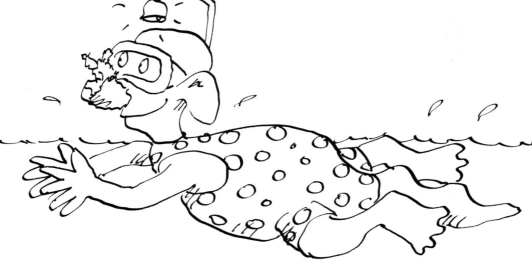

November 12

William the Poet

In the story William The Globetrotter, Miss Milton of the Educational Play Guild asks all the children to choose a bird and write a poem about it. She gives this example:

"About the garden I do flit,
Tom-tit I am, I am tom-tit."

William Brown insists: "I'd sooner be a vulture than any other sort of bird. They know when people are dyin' an' they hover round 'em an' then swoop down an' start eatin' 'em right away."
He then makes up this immortal verse:

"I swoop right down on 'em and then
Dead men I eat, I eat dead men."

RICHMAL CROMPTON, FROM WILLIAM THE SHOWMAN

November 13

Bottoming

Rivulets
of
rain
slide
down
the
windowpane

like
young
beavers
down
an
icy bank

Bottoming
their
first
winter

ROGER MCGOUGH

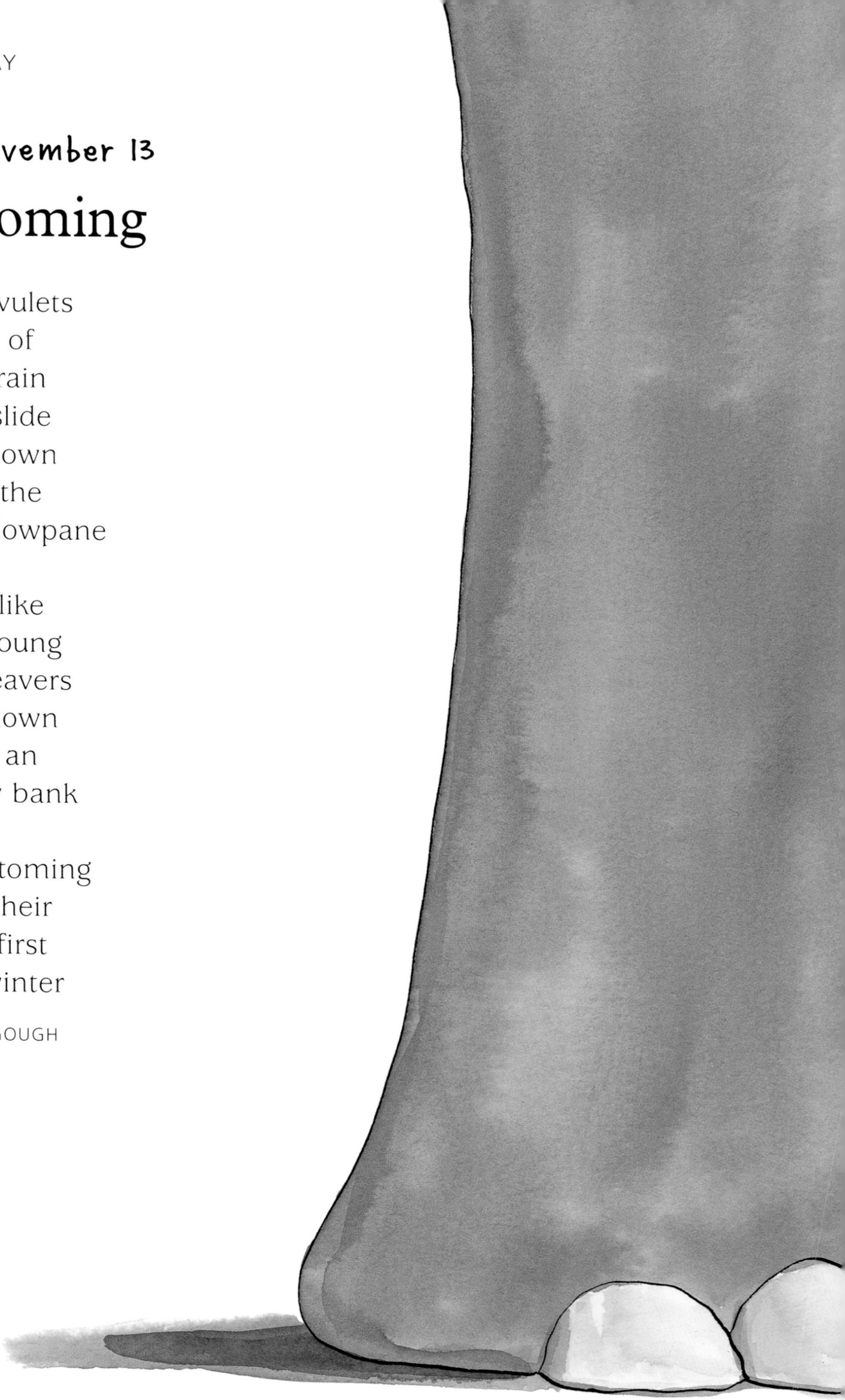

November 14

The Grasshopper and the Elephant

Way down south where bananas grow
Grasshopper stepped on Elephant's toe.
Elephant said, with tears in his eyes:
"Pick on somebody your own size!"

ANON

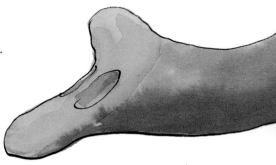

November 15

The Great Figure

Among the rain
and lights
I saw the figure 5
in gold
on a red
firetruck
moving
tense
unheeded
to gong clangs
siren howls
and wheels rumbling
through the dark city.

WILLIAM CARLOS WILLIAMS

November 16

The Shade Catchers

I think they were about as high
As haycocks are. They went running by
Catching bits of shade in the sunny street:
'I've got one,' cried sister to brother,
    I've got two.' 'Now I've got another.'
But scudding away on their little bare feet,
They left the shade in the sunny street.

CHARLOTTE MEW

November 17

Little Mary

I've got a little farm, and I've got a little house,
And I've got a many pretty little milking cows;
I've got a little dog and I've got a little nag
And I've got a little money in a silken bag.
My heart is ever light, yes, as light as light can be
And they call me Little Mary,
Little Mary of the Dee.

ANON

November 18

The City Mouse
and The Garden Mouse

The city mouse lives in a house;
The garden mouse lives in a bower,
He's friendly with the frogs and toads,
And sees the pretty plants in flower.

The city mouse eats bread and cheese;
The garden mouse eats what he can;
We will not grudge him seeds and stocks,
Poor little timid furry man.

CHRISTINA ROSSETTI

249

November 19

from Pleasant Things

'Tis sweet to hear the watch dog's honest bark
Bay deep-mouth'd welcome as we draw near home;
'Tis sweet to know there is an eye will mark
Our coming, and look brighter when we come.

GEORGE GORDON BYRON

November 20

The Ibisters at Home

Mr Ibister, and Betsy his sister,
Resolved upon giving a treat;
    So letters they write,
     Their friends to invite,
To their house in Great Camomile Street.

ANON

November 21

Upon a Snail

She goes but softly, but she goeth sure,
    She stumbles not, as stronger creatures do;
Her journey's shorter, so she may endure
    Better than they which do much further go.

She makes no noise, but stilly seizeth on
    The flower or herb appointed for her food;
The which she quietly doth feed upon,
    While others range, and glare, but find no good.

And though she doth but very softly go,
    However slow her pace be, yet 'tis sure;
And certainly they that do travel so,
    The prize which they do aim at, they procure.

JOHN BUNYAN

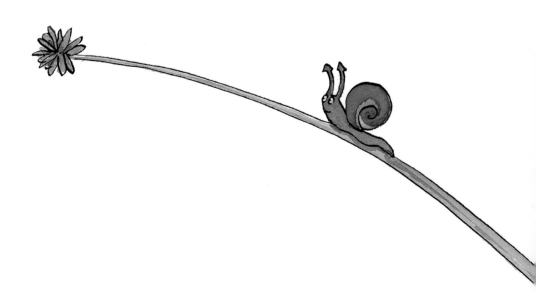

November 22

Little Trotty Wagtail

Little trotty wagtail, he went in the rain,
And tittering tottering sideways, he near got straight again,
He stooped to get a worm, and look'd up to catch a fly,
And then he flew away e're his feathers they were dry.

Little trotty wagtail, he waddled in the mud,
And left his little footmarks trample, where he would.
He waddled in the water-pudge, and waggle went his tail,
And chirrup up his wings to dry upon the garden rail.

Little trotty wagtail, you nimble all about,
And in the dimpling water-pudge you waddle in and out,
Your home is nigh at hand, and in the warm pigsty,
So little Master Wagtail, I'll bid you a good-bye.

JOHN CLARE

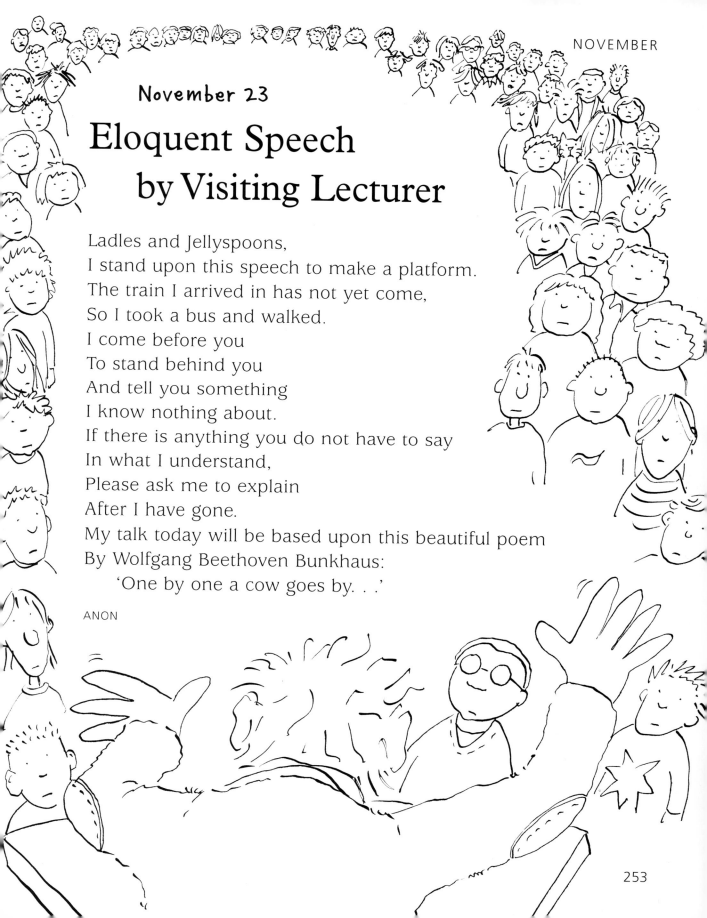

November 23

Eloquent Speech by Visiting Lecturer

Ladles and Jellyspoons,
I stand upon this speech to make a platform.
The train I arrived in has not yet come,
So I took a bus and walked.
I come before you
To stand behind you
And tell you something
I know nothing about.
If there is anything you do not have to say
In what I understand,
Please ask me to explain
After I have gone.
My talk today will be based upon this beautiful poem
By Wolfgang Beethoven Bunkhaus:
    'One by one a cow goes by. . .'

ANON

November 24

Inuit Lullaby (from Greenland)

It's my fat baby
I feel in my hood,
Oh, how heavy he is!
Ya ya! Ya ya!

When I turn my head
He smiles at me, my baby,
Hidden deep in my hood,
Oh, how heavy he is!
Ya ya! Ya ya!

How pretty he is when he smiles
With his two teeth, like a little walrus!
Oh, I'd rather my baby were heavy,
So long as my hood is full!

ANON

November 25

Munchski

On Nevski Bridge a Russian stood
Chewing his beard for lack of food.
Said he, "It's tough this stuff to eat
But a darn sight better than shredded wheat!"

ANON

November 26

The Smiling Villain

Forth from his den to steal he stole,
His bags of chink he chunk,
And many a wicked smile he smole,
And many a wink he wunk.

ANON

255

November 27

Whisky Frisky the Squirrel

Whisky Frisky,
Hipperty hop,
Up he goes
To the tree top!

Whirly, twirly,
Round and round,
Down he scampers
To the ground.

Furly, curly,
What a tail,
Tall as a feather,
Broad as a snail.

Where's his supper?
In the shell.
Snappy, cracky,
Out it fell.

ANON

November 28

When I Was a Little Girl

When I was a little girl about seven years old,
I hadn't got a petticoat to keep me from the cold;
So I went into Darlington, that pretty little town,
And there I bought a petticoat, a cloak and a gown.

I went into the woods and built me a kirk,
And all the birds of the air they helped me to work;
The hawk with his long claws pulled down the stone,
And the dove with her rough bill brought me them home.

The parrot was the clergyman, the peacock was the clerk,
The bullfinch played the organ, and we made merry work.

ANON

(a kirk is a church)

November 29

from Thanksgiving Day

Over the river and through the wood,
      To grandfather's house we go;
      The horse knows the way
      To carry the sleigh
Through the white and drifted snow.

Over the river and through the wood, –
With a clear blue winter sky,
      The dogs do bark
      And children hark
As we go jingling by.

Over the river, and through the wood –
      Now grandmother's cap I spy!
      Hurrah for the fun!
      Is the pudding done?
Hurrah for the pumpkin pie!

L. MARIA CHILD

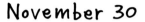

November 30

Skip to my Lou

Hey hey, skip to my lou,
Hey hey, skip to my lou,
Hey hey, skip to my lou,
Skip to my lou my darling.

Lost my partner, what'll I do?
Lost my partner, what'll I do?
Lost my partner, what'll I do?
Skip to my lou my darling.
Hey hey . . .

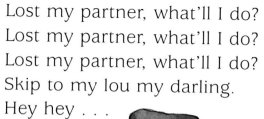

I'll get another one prettier than you . . .

Little red wagon painted blue . . .

Flies in the buttermilk, two by two . . .

Flies in the sugar bowl, shoo, shoo, shoo . . .

Cat's in the cream jar, what'll I do?
Cat's in the cream jar, what'll I do?
Cat's in the cream jar, what'll I do?
Skip to my lou my darling.

Hey hey . . .

ANON

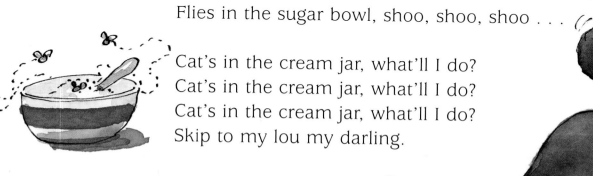

259

December 1

Misfortunes Never Come Singly

Making toast at the fireside,
Nurse fell in the grate and died;
And what makes it ten times worse,
All the toast was burnt with nurse.

HARRY GRAHAM

December 2

Squirrel

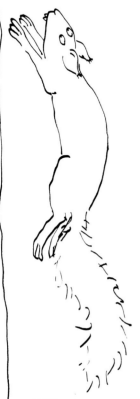

With a rocketing rip
Squirrel will zip
Up a tree-bole
As if down a hole.

He jars to a stop
With tingling ears.
he has two gears:
Freeze and top.

Then up again, plucky
As a jockey
Galloping a Race-
-Horse into space.

TED HUGHES

December 3

Winter Variations

GRASSHOPPERS
Grasshoppers bending blades of grass
Tomorrow will be coated in snow,

However much you want them to stay
The wind will snatch their songs away.

LEAVES
I heard the trees whispering, each tongue was a leaf,
And what they were whispering was, 'Stop, thief!'

Behind them Jack Frost was hurrying away.
In his hands each leaf had begun to decay.

BEES
Flightless bees, numbed by cold,
Leave winding trails in the sparkling frost,
Winter's a maze in which they're lost.

GOLDFISH
Beneath a sheet of milky ice,
Transformed by a wintry wand,

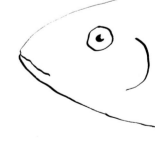

I saw phantom goldfish floating
Like sunken treasure in the pond.

BRIAN PATTEN

December 4

She Walks in Beauty

She walks in beauty, like the night
    Of cloudless climes and starry skies;
And all that's best of dark and bright
    Meet in her aspect and her eyes:
Thus mellowed to that tender light
    Which heaven to gaudy day denies.

GEORGE GORDON BYRON

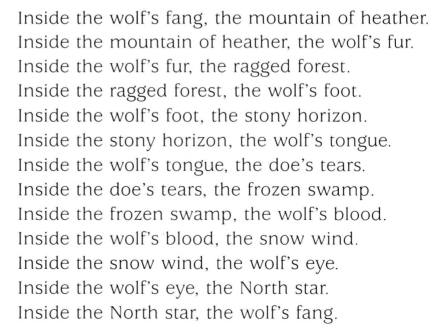

December 5

Amulet

Inside the wolf's fang, the mountain of heather.
Inside the mountain of heather, the wolf's fur.
Inside the wolf's fur, the ragged forest.
Inside the ragged forest, the wolf's foot.
Inside the wolf's foot, the stony horizon.
Inside the stony horizon, the wolf's tongue.
Inside the wolf's tongue, the doe's tears.
Inside the doe's tears, the frozen swamp.
Inside the frozen swamp, the wolf's blood.
Inside the wolf's blood, the snow wind.
Inside the snow wind, the wolf's eye.
Inside the wolf's eye, the North star.
Inside the North star, the wolf's fang.

TED HUGHES

December 6

The Colorado Trail

Eyes like the morning star,
Cheek like a rose,
Laura was a pretty girl,
Godalmighty knows.

Weep, all you little rains,
Wail, winds, wail,
All along, along, along,
The Colorado trail.

ANON

December 7

The Horseman

I heard a horseman
    Ride over the hill;
The moon shone clear,
The night was still;
His helm was silver,
    And pale was he;
And the horse he rode
    Was of ivory.

WALTER DE LA MARE

December 8

She Moved Through the Fair

My young love said to me, 'My brothers won't mind,
And my parents won't slight you for your lack of kind.'
Then she stepped away from me, and this she did say,
'It will not be long, love, till our wedding day.'

She stepped away from me and she moved through the fair,
And fondly I watched her go here and go there,
Then she went her way homeward with one star awake,
As the swan in the evening moves over the lake.

The people were saying no two were e'er wed
But one had a sorrow that never was said,
And I smiled as she passed with her goods and her gear,
And that was the last that I saw of my dear.

I dreamt it last night that my young love came in,
So softly she entered, her feet made no din;
She came close beside me, and this she did say,
'It will not be long, love, till our wedding day.'

PADRAIC COLUM

December 9

My Little Dogs

I had a little dog,
His name was Pop,
Every time he ran
His ears went flop.

I had a little dog,
His name was Trot,
He held up his tail
All tied in a knot.

I had another dog,
His name was Blue,
When he saw a squirrel
He just about flew.

Now I have a dog,
His name is Rover.
When he wags his tail,
He waggles all over.

ANON

December 10

from Twinkle Twinkle Little Star

Twinkle, twinkle, little star,
How I wonder what you are!
Up above the world so high,
Like a diamond in the sky.

When the blazing sun is gone,
When he nothing shines upon,
Then you show your little light,
Twinkle, twinkle all the night.

JANE TAYLOR

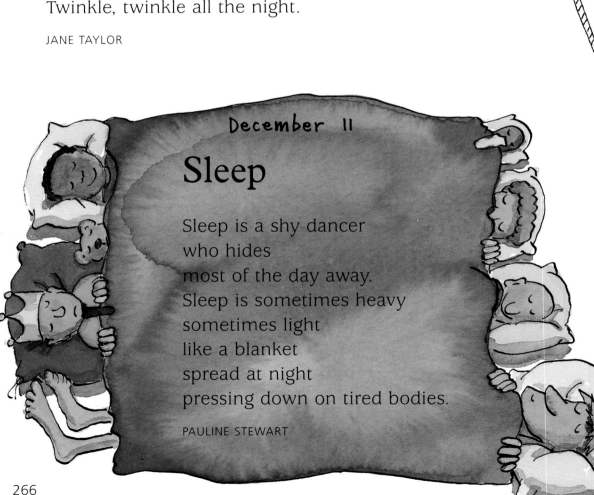

December 11

Sleep

Sleep is a shy dancer
who hides
most of the day away.
Sleep is sometimes heavy
sometimes light
like a blanket
spread at night
pressing down on tired bodies.

PAULINE STEWART

December 12

Useful Insult

Your face looks like a coffee-pot,
Your nose looks like the spout.
Your mouth looks like the fireplace
With the ashes tooken out.

ANON

December 13

from The Wind and the Moon

Said the Wind to the Moon, 'I will blow you out;
    You stare
    In the air
    Like a ghost in a chair,
Always looking what I am about –
I hate to be watched; I'll blow you out.'

The Wind blew hard, and out went the Moon.
    So deep
    On a heap
    Of clouds to sleep,
Down lay the Wind, and slumbered soon,
Muttering low, 'I've done for that Moon.'

GEORGE MACDONALD

December 14

Give Yourself a Hug

Give yourself a hug
when you feel unloved

Give yourself a hug
when people put on airs
to make you feel a bug

Give yourself a hug
when everyone seems to give you
a cold-shoulder shrug

Give yourself a hug –
a big big hug

And keep on singing,
'Only one in a million like me
Only one in a million-billion-trillion-zillion
like me.'

GRACE NICHOLS

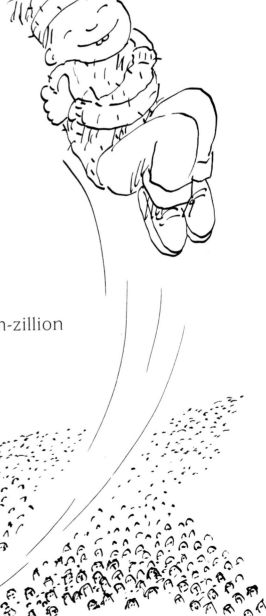

December 15

The Owl

When cats run home and light is come,
   And dew is cold upon the ground,
And the far-off stream is dumb,
   And the whirring sail goes round,
   And the whirring sail goes round;
     Alone and warming his five wits,
     The white owl in the belfry sits.

When merry milkmaids click the latch,
   And rarely smells the new-mown hay,
And the cock hath sung beneath the thatch
   Twice or thrice his roundelay,
   Twice or thrice his roundelay;
     Alone and warming his five wits,
     The white owl in the belfry sits.

ALFRED TENNYSON

December 16

A Surprise Parcel

Hairy green string
Blobs of purple sealing-wax
Six postage stamps bearing silver holograms
Of the Snow Queen on an iceberg throne
Muddy brown wrapping paper
Round a soggy heavy oblong cardboard box
When you sway it from side to side
You hear a swishing-swashing sound –
Somebody has sent you a river.

ADRIAN MITCHELL

December 17

Daydream

One day people will touch and talk perhaps easily,
And loving be natural as breathing and warm as sunlight,
And people will untie themselves, as string is unknotted,
Unfold and yawn and stretch and spread their fingers,
Unfurl, uncurl like seaweed returned to the sea,
And work will be simple and swift as a seagull flying,
And play will be casual and quiet as a seagull settling,
And the clocks will stop, and no one will wonder or care or
notice,
And people will smile without reason, even in the winter,
even in the rain.

A. S. J. TESSIMOND

December 18

The Merry-Matanzie

Here we go round the jing-a-ring,
Jing-a-ring, jing-a-ring;
Here we go round the jing-a-ring,
About the merry-matanzie.

Twice about, and then we fall,
Then we fall, then we fall,
Twice about and then we fall,
About the merry-matanzie.

Guess you who the goodman is,
Goodman is, goodman is,
Guess you who the goodman is,
About the merry-matanzie.

Honey is sweet, and so is he,
So is he, so is he,
Honey is sweet and so is he,
About the merry-matanzie.

Now they're married we'll wish them joy,
Wish them joy, wish them joy,
Now they're married we'll wish them joy,
About the merry-matanzie.

ANON

December 19

At the Zoo

There are lions and roaring tigers, and enormous camels
     and things,
There are biffalo-buffalo-bisons, and a great big bear with wings,
There's a sort of a tiny potamus, and a tiny nosserus too –
But *I* gave buns to the elephant when *I* went down to the Zoo!

There are badgers and bidgers and bodgers, and a
Super-in-tendent's House,
There are masses of goats, and a Polar, and different kinds
     of mouse,
And I think there's a sort of a something which is called
     a wallaboo –
But *I* gave buns to the elephant when *I* went down to the Zoo!

If you try to talk to the bison, he never quite understands;
You can't shake hands with a mingo – he doesn't like
     shaking hands.
And lions and roaring tigers hate saying, 'How do you do?' –
But *I* give buns to the elephant when *I* go down to the Zoo!

A. A. MILNE

December 20

Counting Out

I saw a dove
Fly o'er the dam
With silver wings
And golden band.

She lookit east,
She lookit west,
She lookit where
To light on best.

She lighted on
A bank of sand,
To see the cocks
Of Cumberland.

White pudding,
Black trout,
You're out!

ANON

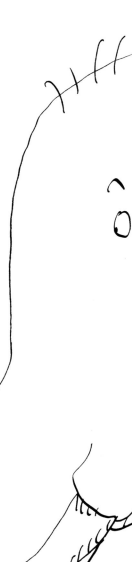

December 21

from The Holly and the Ivy

The holly and the ivy,
When both are full well grown,
Of all the trees that are in the wood,
The holly bears the crown.

O the rising of the sun
And the running of the deer,
The playing of the merry organ,
Sweet singing in the choir.

The holly bears a berry
As red as any blood,
And Mary bore sweet Jesus Christ
For to do poor sinners good.

ANON

December 22

from O Little Town of Bethlehem

O little town of Bethlehem
How still we see thee lie!
Above thy deep and dreamless sleep
The silent stars go by.
Yet in thy dark streets shineth
The everlasting light;
The hopes and fears of all the years
Are met in thee tonight.

PHILIP BROOKS

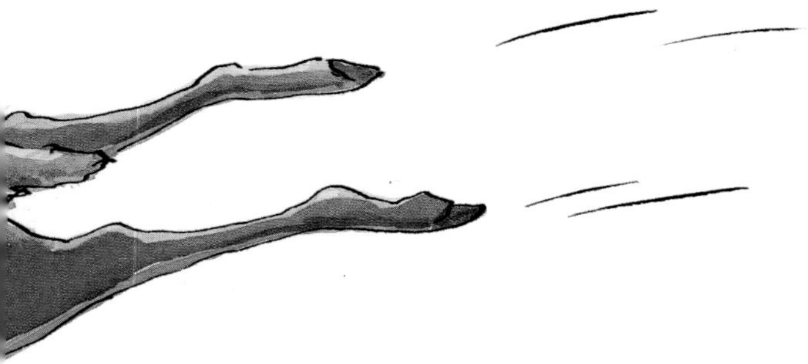

December 23

Blow the Stars Home

Blow the Stars home, Wind, blow the Stars home
'Ere Morning drowns them in golden foam.

ELEANOR FARJEON

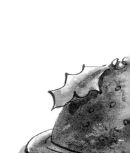

December 24

from **A Visit from St Nicholas**

'Twas the night before Christmas, when all through the house
Not a creature was stirring, not even a mouse;
The stockings were hung by the chimney with care,
In hopes that St. Nicholas soon would be there;
The children were nestled all snug in their beds,
While visions of sugar-plums danced in their heads;
And mamma in her 'kerchief, and I in my cap,
Had just settled our brains for a long winter's nap –
When out on the lawn there arose such a clatter,
I sprang from my bed to see what was the matter.

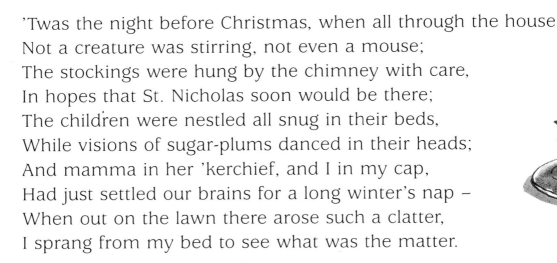

Away to the window I flew like a flash,
Tore open the shutters, and threw up the sash.
The moon, on the breast of the new-fallen snow,
Gave the lustre of midday to objects below;
When, what to my wondering eyes should appear,
But a miniature sleigh and eight tiny reindeer,
With a little old driver, so lively and quick,
I knew in a moment it must be St. Nick.

More rapid than eagles his coursers they came,
And he whistled, and shouted, and called them by name:
'Now, *Dasher*! now, *Dancer*! now, *Prancer*! and *Vixen*!
On, *Comet*! on, *Cupid*! on, *Donner* and *Blitzen*!'

CLEMENT C. MOORE

December 25

I Saw a Stable

I saw a stable low and very bare,
    A little child in a manger.
The oxen knew Him, had Him in their care,
    To men He was a stranger.
The safety of the world was lying there,
    And the world's danger.

MARY COLERIDGE

December 26

The Winter Robin

A suppliant to your window comes,
 Who trusts your faith, and fears no guile:
He claims admittance to your crumbs,
 And reads his passport in your smile.

For cold and cheerless is the day,
 And he has sought the hedges round;
No berry hangs upon the spray,
 Nor worm, nor ant-egg can be found.

Secure his suit will be preferred,
 No fears his slender feet deter;
For sacred is the household bird
 That wears the scarlet stomacher.

CHARLOTTE SMITH

December 27

Night

Stars over snow
    And in the west a planet
Swinging below a star –
    Look for a lovely thing and you will find it,
It is not far –
    It never will be far.

SARA TEASDALE

December 28

The Miser at Christmas

Quoth I, "Here's Christmas come again,
And I no farthing richer!"
Time answered, "Ah, the old old strain!
I prithee pass the pitcher;
Why measure all your good in gold?
No rope of sand is weaker;
'Tis hard to get – 'tis hard to hold;
Come lad, fill up your beaker."

MARK LEMON

December 29

Benediction

Thanks to the ear
that someone may hear

Thanks to seeing
that someone may see

Thanks to feeling
that someone may feel

Thanks to touch
that one may be touched

Thanks to flowering of white moon
and spreading shawl of black night
holding villages and cities together

JAMES BERRY

December 30

from The Way Through the Woods

They shut the road through the woods
Seventy years ago.
Weather and rain have undone it again,
And now you would never know
There was once a road through the woods
Before they planted the trees.
It is underneath the coppice and heath,
And the thin anemones.
Only the keeper sees
That, where the ring-dove broods,
And the badgers roll at ease,
There was once a road through the woods.

RUDYARD KIPLING

December 31

from Ring Out – Ring In

Ring out wild bells to the wild sky,
The flying cloud, the frosty light;
The year is dying in the night;
Ring out, wild bells, and let him die.

Ring out the old, ring in the new,
Ring, happy bells, across the snow
The year is going, let him go.

ALFRED TENNYSON

Prospero the Magician Speaks

Our revels now are ended. These our actors,
As I foretold you, were all spirits and
Are melted into air, into thin air:
And, like the baseless fabric of this vision,
The cloud-capp'd towers, the gorgeous palaces,
The solemn temples, the great globe itself,
Yea, all which it inherit, shall dissolve
And, like this insubstantial pageant faded,
Leave not a rack behind. We are such stuff
As dreams are made on, and our little life
Is rounded with a sleep.

WILLIAM SHAKESPEARE, FROM *THE TEMPEST*

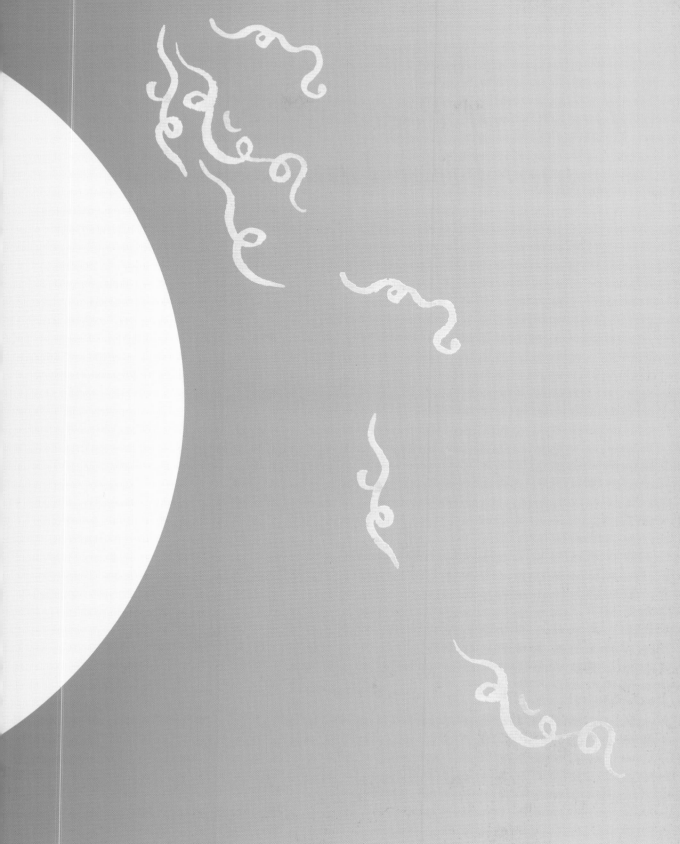

Index of Poets and First Lines

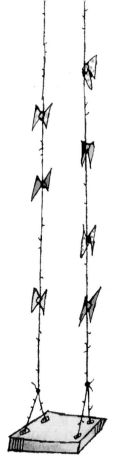

Acknowledgements

'The Song of the Black Bryony Fairy' from FLOWER FAIRIES OF THE AUTUMN by Cicely Mary Barker. Copyright © the Estate of Cicely Mary Barker 1926, 1944. Reproduced with kind permission of Frederick Warne & Co.; 'And God Said to the Little Boy' from TO AYLSHAM FAIR by George Barker, reprinted by permission of Faber and Faber; 'What on Earth Are You Doing Here, Marvellous Mouse' from RUNES AND RHYMES AND TUNES AND CHIMES by George Barker, reprinted by permission of Faber and Faber; 'The Yak' reprinted by permission of The Peters Fraser and Dunlop Group Limited on behalf of the Estate of Hilaire Belloc; 'Sir Christopher Wren' reproduced with permission of Curtis Brown Ltd, London, on behalf of the Estate of E. C. Bentley © the Estate of E. C. Bentley; 'The Barkday Party' and 'Benediction' reprinted by permission of The Peters Fraser and Dunlop Group Limited on behalf of: © James Berry; 'Sun-a-Shine, Rain-a-Fall' © Valerie Bloom 2001, reprinted with permission of Cambridge University Press; 'I had a little dog' © Frances Cornford reproduced by permission of Enitharmon Press; 'William the Poet' from WILLIAM THE SHOWMAN © Richmal Crompton, reproduced in association with Macmillan Children's Books, London; 'The Tide in the River' and 'Blow the Stars Home' © Eleanor Farjeon, from SILVER SAND AND SNOW, reprinted with permission from David Higham Associates; Robert Frost 'Stopping by Woods on a Snowy Evening' and 'The Pasture' © the Estate of Robert Frost, the Editor Edward Connery Lathem, and Jonathan Cape as publisher; 'Young Henry and Mary' and 'The Penny Fiddle' © Robert Graves, reprinted by permission of Carcanet Press Ltd.; 'St Francis and the Birds' from DEATH OF A NATURALIST by Seamus Heaney, reprinted by permission of Faber and Faber; 'Marigolds' from THE PHANTOM LOLLIPOP LADY © 1986 Adrian Henri. Published by Methuen Children's Books Ltd, an imprint of Egmont Children's Books and used with permission; 'Small, Smaller' © Russell Hoban, from THE PEDALLING MAN, reprinted with permission from David Higham Associates; 'Stupidity Street' from COLLECTED POEMS © Ralph Hodgson, reprinted with permission from Macmillan; 'Fantails' and 'Squirrel' from THE CAT AND THE CUCKOO by Ted Hughes, 'Amulet' from MOONBELLS AND OTHER POEMS by Ted Hughes, reprinted by permission of Faber and Faber 'The Common Cormorant' reproduced with permission of Curtis Brown Ltd, London, on behalf of the Estate of Christopher Isherwood. © the Estate of Christopher Isherwood 1966; 'They Shut the Road Through the Woods' © Rudyard Kipling, reprinted by permission of A. P. Watt Ltd on behalf of The National Trust for Places of Historical Interest or Historical Beauty; 'The Hare', 'The Bandog', 'Silver', 'Please to Remember', 'The Horseman' and 'Tartary' © Walter de la Mare, reproduced with permission from The Literary Trustees of Walter de la Mare, and the Society of Authors as their representative; 'Cargoes' © John Masefield, reproduced with permission from the Society of Authors as the literary representative of the Estate of John Masefield; 'he who owns the whistle, rules the world' reprinted by permission of the Peters Fraser and Dunlop Group Limited on behalf of: Roger McGough ©: Roger McGough 1976; 'Fame' reprinted by permission of the Peters Fraser and Dunlop Group Limited on behalf of: Roger McGough ©: Roger McGough 1987; 'a cat, a horse and the sun' reprinted by permission of the Peters Fraser and Dunlop Group Limited on behalf of: Roger McGough ©: Roger McGough 1989; 'A Good Poem' reprinted by permission of the Peters Fraser and Dunlop Group Limited on behalf of: Roger McGough ©: Roger McGough 1976, 'Bottoming' reprinted by permission of the Peters Fraser and Dunlop Group Limited on behalf of: Roger McGough ©: Roger McGough 1987; 'At the Zoo' and 'The Christening' from WHEN WE WERE VERY YOUNG © A. A. Milne. Copyright under the Berne Convention. Published by Methuen, an imprint of Egmont Children's Books Limited, London, and used with permission; 'The Loch Ness Monster's Song' © Edwin Morgan, reprinted by permission of Carcanet Press Ltd; 'Give Yourself a Hug' reproduced with permission of Curtis Brown Limited, London, on behalf of Grace Nichols. © Grace Nichols 1994; 'Daddy Fell Into the Pond' © Alfred Noyes, reproduced with permission of the Society of Authors as the Literary Representative of the Estate of Alfred Noyes; 'Squeezes' and 'Snodding' from GARGLING WITH JELLY' by Brian Patten (Viking 1985) © Brian Patten 1985, reproduced by permission of Penguin Books Limited; 'Ten Angels Alone on Trapezes' and 'Winter Variations' © Brian Patten 1990. Reproduced by permission of the author c/o Rogers Coleridge and White Limited, 20 Powis Mews, London, W11 1JN; 'All Over the Lilac Brine' and 'What a Day it's Been' from RHYMES WITHOUT REASON © 1974 by Mervyn Peake. First published 1944 by Eyre and Spottiswoode Limited and